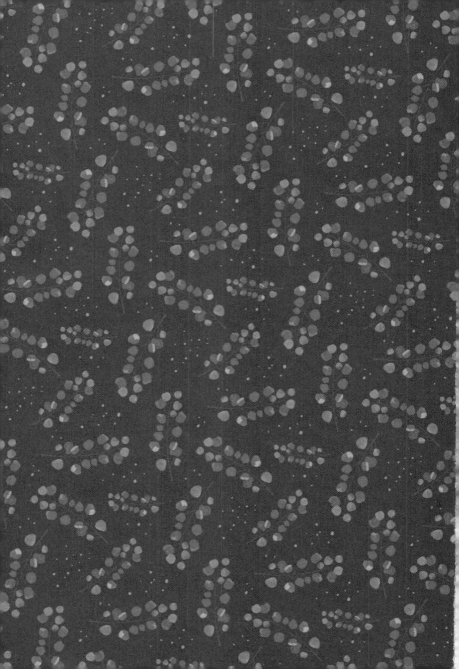

To

Jane

From

Jada

Date

01 - 27 - 2020

Happy Birthday!

Be STILL

90 Devotions
— for the —
Hopeful Heart

CLEERE CHERRY

DaySpring
LIVE YOUR FAITH

Be Still: 90 Devotions for the Hopeful Heart
Copyright © 2019 Cleere Cherry. All rights reserved.
First Edition, October 2019

Published by:

DaySpring

P.O. Box 1010
Siloam Springs, AR 72761
dayspring.com

Scripture quotations marked ESV are taken from the ESV Bible® (The Holy Bible,
English Standard Version®) copyright ©2001 by Crossway Bibles, a publishing
ministry of Good News Publishers. Used by permission. All rights reserved.

Scriptures quotations marked NIV are taken from the Holy Bible, New International
Version®, NIV®. Copyright © 1973, 1978, 1984, 2011 by Biblica, Inc.® Used by permission
of Zondervan. All rights reserved worldwide. www.zondervan.com. The "NIV" and
"New International Version" are trademarks registered in the United States Patent
and Trademark Office by Biblica, Inc.®

Scripture quotations marked THE MESSAGE are taken from THE MESSAGE,
copyright © 1993, 1994, 1995, 1996, 2000, 2001, 2002 by Eugene H. Peterson. Used
by permission of NavPress. All rights reserved. Represented by Tyndale House
Publishers, Inc.

Scripture quotations marked NLT are taken from the Holy Bible, New Living
Translation, copyright © 1996, 2004, 2007 by Tyndale House Foundation. Used by
permission of Tyndale House Publishers, Inc., Carol Stream, Illinois 60188. All rights
reserved.

Scripture quotations marked NASB are taken from the NEW AMERICAN STANDARD
BIBLE®, Copyright © 1960,1962,1963,1968,1971,1972,1973,1975,1977,1995 by The
Lockman Foundation. Used by permission.

Scripture quotations marked NKJV are taken from the New King James Version®.
Copyright © 1982 by Thomas Nelson. Used by permission. All rights reserved.

Scripture quotations marked GNT are from the Good News Translation in Today's
English Version- Second Edition Copyright © 1992 by American Bible Society. Used
by Permission.

Printed in China
Prime: 89895
ISBN: 978-1-68408-623-8

Contents

Introduction

*May the God of hope fill you with all joy
and peace in believing,
so that by the power of the Holy Spirit
you may abound in hope.*
ROMANS 15:13 ESV

Stillness...and Hope. Correlating the two seems confusing at first; why is one necessary for the other? However, the more we dive into what stillness really looks like and what comes from spending time with God, the more we understand that stillness invites hope to reside permanently in our heart.

We want to be people of solitude and stamina. We want to be both focused and interruptible to Jesus. We want to be intentional in our schedules while also allowing for margin. We want to be people who remain in a posture of peace while remaining aware of the urgency to share God's love. Following Jesus does not require us to compromise any part of something good; rather, it is our connection with Him that directs us in the way that is all things good. As we walk in step with Him and learn to trust Him on our journey, we are able to take part in His miracles.

Hopeful hearts are cultivated through stillness with our Creator. As we see the grandeur of the sky and walk the shoreline of the ocean, our eyes are opened to His sovereignty and majesty. The more we understand the heart of our Father, the more our own heart will walk in hope no matter our circumstance. We are here for a short while, but His kingdom is forever. And the only way to make the present *significant* is to invest in what is forever.

I hope this devotional serves as a continual recalibration for you wherever you are in life. Our hope as children of God is always present, as it is anchored in His presence. Where we go, He goes. Where we stay, He stays. As we travel about our days and navigate this thing called life, may we stop and be with Him. We will never waste a moment doing so. When our days are demanding or our world feels chaotic, let us draw back and rest in the shadow of His wings. Let us drink from His well, regain our energy, and be reminded of our eternal hope and joy in Jesus.

Be still, child.

In the Hands of Hope

This is how we know that we belong to the truth and how we set our hearts at rest in His presence.

1 JOHN 3:19 NIV

We try so hard to make things happen on our own, don't we? In our timing. The way we like it. How we've planned it in our mind. In our mixing-up of roles, we often forget His power. We think we have to "wake Him up" to our reality when the waves feel too big and inform Him of our dreams when the waters seem stagnant.

But He is God.

He knows our desires and where we would like to go.

He knows our shortcomings and what might prevent us from getting there.

He knows our potential and the possibilities that lie within us.

He also knows the timing of how it all comes together—how things will shift into place, how certain doors will close and unexpected ones will open, how stubborn we can get when we believe in something, and how fearful we allow our heart to get when vulnerability calls our name.

Yet even though He knows all, He gives us grace when we think *we* do. It's like a child pretending to drive a car while sitting in a parent's lap, gripping the steering wheel, wide-eyed and ready, believing they're in control—when in reality, their loving parent has control of the wheel the entire time. The child's feet dangle in midair as the parent presses the gas and the brake. They chuckle that their child believes the verbal command "Go faster" actually makes the car travel at higher speeds.

Isn't this us, white-knuckling the wheel, believing we are in control, while our Father smiles and keeps us on course?

We do not have to worry that our God is One who doesn't know what we want or need. Or that He's boring, stingy, or stale and won't provide it. Or even that His timeline is a little behind what our mind tells us is the socially acceptable timeline. Our desires are not far from His mind.

He is mighty. Trust what He knows and follow where He goes. Remember His hands—they have us. And haven't we learned? His hands do not fail.

Dear Jesus, thank You for being patient in our stubbornness and forgetfulness. Remind our heart that Your will is perfect and true. You know us intricately, and You lead us perfectly. We place today in Your hands. In Jesus's name, amen.

Removing the Busy Badge

The God of peace will soon crush Satan under your feet.
The grace of our Lord Jesus be with you.
ROMANS 16:20 NIV

It's hard to get a handle on time, isn't it? It passes more quickly with each year. The days seemed longer "back then." It felt a little easier to stay in our present, with our mind focusing on exactly where we were, who we were with, and what we were doing.

But the clock has not changed any, other than the fact that it has become a little square on our Apple watch instead of the ticking circle in the elementary school classroom. Each moment is as available to soak up today as it was then; it's just that we are less available.

We have nurtured the myth that busyness equates to value and that a hurried lifestyle means an important life. But stacking our demands like dominoes and overcommitting ourselves does not make us popular or powerful. It only makes us less purposeful.

Busy is not a badge of honor. At the end of our life, we will not want to be remembered for how many e-mails we typed or how many coffee dates we were able to fit into a month's time line. We will have wanted to have been intentional with those we love and selfless in those we serve.

We can slow it down. Nothing will catch on fire. Watch as Jesus multiplies our time and gives us the ability to pursue what matters most in each moment.

As we plan our days, why don't we consult our heavenly Father on how to do so? Instead of claiming "busy," let's change it to "full." And when we begin to question our importance, let's ask Him for reminders of who we are.

Dear Jesus, thank You for the value you have placed over every one of Your children. We do not have to earn our significance, for You already claimed us by name. We will walk in that truth today knowing that You desire our time to be marked with intentionality rather than busyness. In Jesus's name, amen.

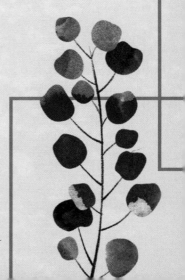

The Power of Our Potential

I pray that your hearts will be flooded with light
so that you can understand the confident hope
He has given to those He called—His holy people
who are His rich and glorious inheritance.

EPHESIANS 1:18 NLT

Our potential—do we really have any idea what it is? Or what it could look like?

Even with the ways we perceive life will change or imagine the possibilities that could happen when we dream big and fly high, we still tend to undermine our abilities and place ourselves in a box.

We want to believe for the impossible, step into the unknown, and trust God completely in His Word, but we want to do these things in ways that do not force us out of our comfort zones.

Friends, if we really and truly understood the mightiness and grace of the Father, our lives would look different in every way. But to know *how* they would look different, we have to understand the heart of our heavenly Father.

Scripture states, "Your hearts will be flooded

with light so that you can understand the confident hope...." When our heart is flooded with light, which is the truth of His Word, we no longer question our ability to show up—nor do we need the affirmation of everyone around us before we enter our potential. When our heart is flooded with light, we begin to step into the person He has always seen us as—holy, beloved, and pure...full of complete joy and soaked in creativity, passion, and kindness. This process is not glorious because of the earthly riches it will provide but because of the way it refines our heart.

How are we doing with this? Do we read Scripture as though it is truly written for us and about us, or does it feel distant and confusing? It is time to step into these places we know our feet have been created to go and then walk in the confident hope that our inheritance offers. Our potential is unmatched, world-changing, and certain, but we must let the light flood our heart and hope guide our footsteps. It is time to fully believe.

Dear Jesus, thank You for being a sure and loving Father. You believe in us, and You desire to use us in mighty ways. Help us break out of our socially acceptable boxes and run hard after You. We want to break the mold. In Jesus's name, amen.

He Knows Life Is a Lot

Truly my soul finds rest in God;
my salvation comes from Him.
PSALM 62:1 NIV

"Unclench your teeth. Take your tongue off the top of your mouth. Release the tension in your hands." As the yoga instructor mentioned each thing, I thought to myself. "What? I didn't realize I was doing these to begin with!"

Isn't that so often how we approach so much of life, though? We do what we have always done simply because we have always done it. We go at breakneck speed because we are told we will get behind or be subpar if we choose our own pace. This accelerated rhythm not only affects our mental capacity, spiritual awareness, and emotional well-being, but it physically causes our body to be in defense mode. It often takes us being still to realize how frantic we have become.

The reality is, we all have a lot going on. We have a lot to manage, a lot to balance, a lot to understand, and even a lot to surrender. But it also probably feels like a lot because we never slow down long enough to set it down and rest our shoulders. We assume that whatever we want to remain in our life, we must deal with all at once. We cannot miss out, mess up, or miss it. We feel the need to be the perfect friend, husband/wife, family member, leader all while painting the picture that we understand vulnerability. What we share with others still remains the socially acceptable answer because if they really—like, really—knew our level of crazy? Well, it is just too much. So we juggle.

We forget to breathe and remind ourselves of the bigger picture. His Word has informed us that we have been placed exactly where we are, with what we have, "for such a time as this." All the balls in the air can wait for a moment. Because if the juggler forgets that underneath them is a net to catch them, they will live in constant fear of falling.

He knows we have a lot. But nothing in our hand is worth compromising the hope in our heart.

Let's unclench our teeth, remove our tongue from the top of our mouth, release the tension in our hands, and be okay with just *being*.

Dear Jesus, thank You for being a God of peace. Help us to be thankful for the blessings and the burdens we have, trusting that You are our Help and Provider. We are not crazy; we are human, and You love us more than anything. Remind our soul of that. In Jesus's name, amen.

Red Light, Green Light

The Lord is not slow in keeping His promise,
as some understand slowness.
Instead He is patient with you,
not wanting anyone to perish,
but everyone to come to repentance.

II PETER 3:9 NIV

Remember the game we used to play growing up called "Red Light, Green Light"? Everyone stands in a line, and when the person at the front says to the group, "Green light," all run forward. When they say, "Red light," the runners stop. The first person to reach the front wins the game, so the point is to sprint as fast as humanly possible when the green light is given so that ground is gained. The catch? When the red light is given, whoever is still moving is automatically disqualified. The desire to cross the finish line becomes so tangible and appealing that we begin to compromise our ability to receive direction. We stop and go so often that we find our feet traveling forth when the red light is signaled, and our effort becomes futile.

Isn't this similar to our spiritual walk on this earth when we come to a red light in life? The outcome has become our obsession, so any red light that stands in our way is considered an obstacle, an unwelcome interruption, and certainly not a moment we will "lean into the stillness."

But ponder for a moment—what would God's instructions sound like? He would probably say "Green light" when the world says "Red light" and vice versa, knowing that we often do not know when we need to catch our breath. He would probably remind us that while it seems like a race, those around us are not our competition. He would go against the rules and let us keep playing even after we ran a red light, covering our mishap with grace and restarting our engine. His focus would not be our finish time but rather on our gaze: are we looking to Him?

As we go about our day today, let us trust the signals He gives, diligently running after green and patiently stopping upon red. Let us invite the stillness as it reinvigorates our soul and energizes our body, preparing us for the next green light.

Dear Jesus, thank You for being a God of peace with perfect timeliness and patience. We trust Your direction even when it looks different than what we were expecting. Help us to lean into stillness and take a deep breath. You are good. In Jesus's name, amen.

Just Passing Through

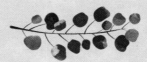

For we know that if the tent that is our earthly home is destroyed, we have a building from God, a house not made with hands, eternal in the heavens.

II CORINTHIANS 5:1 ESV

The more "life" we experience, the more we learn that grief comes in many forms. It can come at any moment. It offers no manners, asking when we think our heart could better handle the tough moments. It spares no one, seizing the opportunity to strike us all to our knees.

And in these moments, the ones when we believe the world truly stops, we are jolted out of our reality. Nothing feels in control. Everything feels fragile.

We deeply question, "Lord, where are You? Why?" We search the index of possibilities and wonder why this had to be. Life as we know it will always look different. While the passing of a loved one, a divorce, or extreme financial hardship are moments that automatically can be registered as grief, sometimes grief looks a lot different. Sometimes it looks like abandoning our preconceived timeline for getting married, letting go of a relationship that had become toxic, or coming face-to-face with consequences we ourselves induced. We often mislabel grief, not fully comprehending the void that is in our life.

But in these moments, our soul recognizes desperation. We grasp the realization that life on earth requires many knee-prints. When uncertainty, fear, and pain become real to us, we more intimately understand that Jesus is our only known. As we cry out to Him in prayer, we begin to see that He is our only Source of peace. These conversations with Him link our hands and keep them interlocked with His. Being close to Him, our spirit witnesses the depth of His love, His grace, and His mercy for us. As our heart aches and our feet stumble, He uses our weariness to show us His glory. Because how else do we get put back together except by His hands?

Moments of grief remind us that we were never meant to get comfortable here. We learn that maybe all this hard stuff is the big arrow that points to our true home with our heavenly Father. We are just passing through. No need to set up a kingdom here or let life convince us that grief is our constant companion. Oh no. Hope is our companion. We, the chosen people of God, can have hopeful hearts.

Dear Jesus, thank You that You are always near, even when our heart is weary or sad. Will You remind us of our forever home? Let the truth of eternity with You permeate our heart with hope and joy. In Jesus's name, amen.

Posture of Peace

*You will keep in perfect peace those whose minds are
steadfast, because they trust in You.*
ISAIAH 26:3 NIV

Have you ever met someone who seemed to have a supernatural ability to be unaffected when life threw them curveballs? They received no warning and yet they never lost their peace or gave up hope.

We probably all have someone who immediately comes to mind. We envy their steadfastness. They challenge our own heart—"Lord, I want whatever that is."

Of all the riches we own and of all the qualities we admire, there is nothing richer than a life of peace. In fact, if we really think about it, when we are striving and reaching and working to attain more, isn't that what we are actually after? We want to wake up, enjoy our days, practice contentment, and know that our heavenly Father is trustworthy. We want to be people of peace, especially when the unexpected arises or struggles are present.

Peace is not reserved for pastors, Bible study

leaders, or worship teams. It is God's desire for all of us to experience peace so that we will stand out in today's world. When we spend time being still, allowing our mind to grab hold of truth and not be distracted by what's around us, we give margin for peace to flow within us and from us.

This posture of peace is a decision. Having a posture of peace doesn't mean having an event-free life. We will all face harsh circumstances, tough decisions, and painful events. But God's peace "surpasses all understanding," meaning that we can rest in Him no matter what comes our way. It means carrying His peace inside us. Our desire to have a peaceful life is already God at work.

Today, let's focus on keeping our gaze ahead, allowing our spine to fully strengthen itself in courage and our focus to be on pursuing peace. It is not enough to just believe He is God; we must believe that God wants to be great in us.

Dear Jesus, thank You for the richest gift we could ever ask for in this life—Your peace. When we begin to feel pressured or worried, recalibrate our mind. Your promises are true and Your way is peace. In Jesus's name, amen.

Even the Waves Obey Him

He replied, "You of little faith, why are you so afraid?"
Then He got up and rebuked the winds and the waves,
and it was completely calm. The men were amazed
and asked, "What kind of man is this?
Even the winds and the waves obey Him!"
MATTHEW 8:26–27 NIV

We can all close our eyes and imagine the ocean; it is its own beast, gigantic and mysterious in all it holds. Most of us can remember a time we learned about the power of the waves as we were knocked down and carried by a current we severely underestimated. This image allows us to really picture ourselves in the biblical story of Matthew 8:18–27. Here we are, on a boat in the middle of the sea, with the storm pulsing all around us. Despite our frantic concern, Jesus is lying still, sleeping. We wake Him and He immediately calms the waves. Stills them, actually. Roaring tidal waves become like glass.

Jesus knew that the disciples needed to physically feel and see His power. Even though their faith had drifted, His authority had not. The disciples were placing their trust in what they could see, but Jesus was asking them to trust in what they could not see.

Jesus, the One who can silence the sea, is watching over us too. How can we not be hopeful? How can we let the bumps so easily discourage us? Belief in Him has never been about the absence or disappearance of storms; it is about the faith to get in the boat and the hope that will guide us until we get home.

When our life feels chaotic or we feel as if God is taking a nap in the middle of our hurricane, let this story remind us of truth. He is not worried, because He is in control. When the rest of the world is calling "mayday" or those around us are unsure, we will take refuge in Him.

Good news for us: the Captain of our ship is also the Creator of the ship and all that surrounds it. Our security is His top priority and our peace His top concern. So remember when the storm comes, He has navigated through many before yours.

Dear Jesus, thank You for telling us of the time You stilled the waves and calmed the storm. Remind our heart that You are our safe place, the Source of our peace. Our eyes are on You. You are mighty in our life, and we trust what You're doing. In Jesus's name, amen.

Knowing the Hope Giver

May the God of hope fill you with all joy
and peace as you trust in Him,
so that you may overflow with hope
by the power of the Holy Spirit.
ROMANS 15:13 NIV

Oftentimes we think that if we could just change our viewpoint, that would be the answer to all our problems. We have been told that perspective is powerful, which is certainly true, but we miss a crucial point. What if instead of searching for a different pair of glasses, we focus on the Hand that is moving us forward? Our route would then become all about who is leading us, trusting the plan of the Guide and His wisdom on this treasure map called life.

God is not holding hope in a jar, choosing to delve out amounts according to our allegiance. He does not desire to ration our supply or "teach us a lesson." Oh no. He is generous beyond belief and yearns for our pursuit of His heart so that we may become more like Him.

Remember, the only way to attain a heavenly

perspective is to spend time with the One who made heaven itself—the One who knows what forever really looks like and what it expects from us now. If we want to share the hope we have found, we must *know* the hope we have found.

Are we hopeful because our life looks as promised, or are we hopeful because we know the Giver of hope and firmly believe that He has our best interests at heart? Life will never keep the same set of circumstances; even in the mundane, our situations evolve and our resources change. This uncertainty can scare us or it can draw us in, searching for our Savior and the security of His character amid the unknown. With the Giver of hope as our guide, we can have the same assuredness in our steps on our hardest and our happiest days.

Lord, thank You for being the Giver of all hope. As we go about our day, remind us that hope is who You are, the very nature of Your being. Let us draw near, spend time with You, and be reassured that because we can trust Your heart, we can always have hope beyond our situations. In Jesus's name, amen.

Change of Pace

Consider the lilies, how they grow:
they neither toil nor spin, yet I tell you,
even Solomon in all his glory was not arrayed like one of
these. But if God so clothes the grass,
which is alive in the field today, and tomorrow is thrown
into the oven, how much more will he clothe you,
O you of little faith!"
LUKE 12:27–28 ESV

Our body naturally responds to and is strengthened by resistance. In our physical journey, we have to change up our routine if we want our muscles to be challenged by our exercise regimen. Our spiritual walk is the same way. Life suggests the "do more, be more" approach, offering very little time to be still. This yields the same rushed rhythm we have grown accustomed to; we are always going and coming, both mentally and physically.

But what if we literally forced our body to slow down? No explanation given to the outside world other than that of self-awareness and spirit-care, if any explanation is even offered. We know resistance will be present, but that means we are experiencing growth.

Would our body respond? This welcomed form of solitude and intentional decision to slow our roll would invite Jesus to take over. Much like when we change up our exercise routine, going against the grain will not come easy. In the moments when the lies start to fill our head, labeling our stillness as laziness, we can invite Jesus to remind us of our new pace. As we force ourselves to stay in one place instead of hopping from here to there, we will experience the freedom to just be with Jesus and experience His kindness.

Jesus never intended His children to travel at breakneck speed and still maintain a mind of peace. He knows that if we can accept the change of pace, we will be shocked at how much our understanding of our purpose follows. The rush-around no longer will cause a rush inside us; it will remind us that our heavenly Father's pace is perfect.

Jesus, thank You for the ability to slow down and be still in You. While You provided us with the body to soar to great heights, You created us to have boundaries that, when crossed, make us weak. Settle our mind when we feel the pressure to speed up, and remind us that You are transforming us. In Jesus's name, amen.

"But if you find yourself experiencing a desire to seek God, we have great news for you: God is already at work in you."

HENRY BLACKABY

Not the World's Hope

But those who hope in the LORD
will renew their strength.
They will soar on wings like eagles;
they will run and not grow weary,
they will walk and not be faint.

ISAIAH 40:31 NIV

Have you ever heard someone say, "I really hope it works out!" or maybe, "I hope everything ends up okay"? While neither statement is negative, this connotation of hope can be extremely fickle. Here, the word "hope" is used as a positive expression—a wishful desire that may or may not come true.

However, biblical hope? The kind that stems from a "hopeful heart" is a hope of confident expectation. The desire is present, but the outcome is also secure. When we "hope in God," we are expressing in absolute certainty our belief that we know He will deliver. We are not wondering and wishing God to show up; we are sure He will make Himself known. It is not positivity, "good vibes," or a wish list; it is a firm stance that determines how we will or will not move forward in a situation. It is hope placed on the One in control versus hope placed in the outcome of our circumstances.

We know very little, see only a smidgen, and have no inclination of what is to come. But our God is everywhere at all times; He is all-powerful, and He knows all things. A hopeful heart is one that is anchored in the true character of God. Hopeful hearts believe God to be who He says He is; they do not waver based on the ebb and flow of what we experience on this earth.

When we hope in God, we are choosing a different way. His way is supernatural, finding renewal when depletion feels imminent. His way allows us to run our race and not worry about the race of others. His way provides us with the divine direction and energy we need to live the abundant life He has called us to. Let us be a people who live in expectation and anticipation of what our God is doing and how He is moving. Let us be a people who do not flake out at the first mention of unforeseen circumstances or who fear the future.

Let us hope like Jesus and show the world what it means to be loved by God.

Dear Jesus, thank You that Your hope is not one that diminishes or discourages us. Your hope is always present because You are always present and You are our hope. Show us how to cling to Your hope. Let us look different than the world. In Jesus's name, amen.

Return to the Reservoir

He who believes in Me, as the Scripture said,
"From his innermost being
will flow rivers of living water."
JOHN 7:38 NASB

What does hope or faith have to do with a reservoir? A reservoir is a base of water that is tapped into and used to supply water to connecting rivers in case the river-water level is low during droughts or dry periods. These reservoirs serve as life rafts, supplying the need during tough seasons. What is our reservoir? When tracking through the wilderness or the lonely times in life, we desperately need that reservoir of hope to kick into gear and help sustain us.

Think about times where our backs have been against the wall and everything seems to be going wrong—where do we turn? If we do not have a supply of hope that we can lean on, our dismal perspective during the wilderness can keep us from seeing Jesus in our circumstances.

When we have this reservoir, this place full of His promises and His teachings, we have a deep well to depend on when we feel broken, bruised, or empty. When evil is done to us, we can deny our human desire to retaliate and dig deep into the well of truth. When temptation knocks or immediate gratification vies for our attention, we can remind our heart of our eternal hope. We can stop, be still, and visit the well. That is the only way our reservoir will be filled, by accessing the center of all wellness and wholeness— the Living Water. When setbacks are experienced, this reservoir is a dependable source that speaks life into our dry bones and assures us that our temporary emotions are not our God-given destiny.

How do we fight for holiness? We dig a deep reservoir and fill it with hope. We do not let our pride determine our need for water, because we know we are nothing without our thirst for Him. We are diligent in our work and faithful in our service, and when our emotions get the best of us? We return to the reservoir and drink again.

Lord, thank You that You are the well that never runs dry. You fill us with strength, lead us in joy, and usher us forward in peace. When we are feeling empty or dissatisfied today, let us return to You. Thank You for being our reservoir, dependable and abundant in all You give. In Jesus's name, amen.

Kneeling in Need

Come, let us worship and bow down,
let us kneel before the LORD our Maker.
PSALM 95:6 NASB

Kneeling, the ultimate display of surrender to authority... Although we would like to say that we assume this position at all times, isn't it often the moments when we have nothing left that we are brought to our knees?

God made us. He knows the presumptive nature of our deceitful heart and that we try to do things ourselves until we are at the point of desperation or breaking. These moments become invitations to assume the position that we were meant to live in— kneeling. There, we are humble, surrendered, and fully dependent on our heavenly Father to show up. And when we do? Our heart is filled with hope. He scoops us up in typical Father fashion and speaks life into our soul.

Don't you think He deeply desires to have this relationship with us not just on a "have-to" basis? As in, we kneel *before* our backs are against the wall, because the record of our life proves that we will never not need Jesus and He will never not be faithful.

What if, in each moment of stress we experience, instead of whipping out our cell phone and calling a confidant, we took that moment to Jesus? It does not have to be big in order for it to be pressing. Those little moments are the ones that eventually add up to be the mountains we fear we cannot climb. But if, one by one, we decide to take them to the throne and address them with the King, our confidence will grow with each step up the mountain.

The greatest way we could ever spend our time is to be in conversation with God. Whether we are the ones talking or the ones listening, it is our kneeling to His authority that opens the gates of heaven to move on our behalf. Learning His heart equips us with the courage we need for all endeavors and the joy we desire to express amid our journey.

And if it is desperation that takes us to our knees? Take heart. The hard times heighten all our senses as we become more aware and dependent upon His presence.

Dear Jesus, thank You that nothing is too big or too small to bring to Your feet. You desire more than anything for us to stop and kneel so that we can be reminded of who You are and who we are in You. We love You and we kneel before You, giving all of ourselves today. In Jesus's name, amen.

FIOS: Figure It Out Syndrome

And I am sure of this, that he who began a good work in you will bring it to completion at the day of Jesus Christ.
PHILIPPIANS 1:6 ESV

Patience. Sure! No problem. Until it requires us to wait on something we really, really want. Or wait for an answer to something we desperately need to know. Or wait on a problem that must quickly go away. Then patience becomes a problem.

Somehow we have convinced ourselves that worrying about something in our life will provide us with the ability, resources, or wisdom to figure it out. Joy is present until we realize that there are many times when the "fix-it method" simply will not work.

Think about a time when life presented a problem and the solution was not obvious. Actually, forget obvious. The solution was nowhere to be found. Would fixating on the issue and becoming consumed with the outcome change the circumstances? No! But we can't seem to help ourselves.

But here is the thing: we cannot assume responsibility or expect to have authority in a position that was never meant to be ours. We can do our best to white-knuckle a controlled grip on life, but it is no secret that we are not the ones in control. The heart was wired with the hope of trusting in God to figure it out, not the other way around.

The sooner we remove this burden from ourselves to be the "fixer," the sooner we can rest in His perfect peace and walk in the fullness of His joy. Our mind will never be able to predict the exciting, adventurous, big life God has for us. Detours will be inevitable and trust will be necessary. The figure-it-out syndrome will have to be replaced with "FIOJ"—Figure It Out, Jesus. An abundant life is a surrendered life, wholly and completely.

And He will figure it out. He always does. Our reliance on Him will provide the freedom and confidence to be exactly who He needs us to be along the way. Our life is His. May we get out of His way and remove the pressure we have placed on ourselves. God is moving on our behalf, and His plans for us are bigger than anything we can imagine.

Dear Jesus, thank You for being the solution to every problem we encounter. You created this world and perfected this life—nothing is outside of You. Help us to relinquish our fears and walk in bravery. We surrender the desire to figure it all out because we know that You are trustworthy and faithful. In Jesus's name, amen.

Vulnerability without Pity

*But to the degree that you share
the sufferings of Christ, keep on rejoicing,
so that also at the revelation of His glory
you may rejoice with exultation.*

I PETER 4:13 NASB

Authenticity has become somewhat trendy. Instagram has provided a platform for people to share "behind-the-scenes footage." It is exciting that our society is embracing this level of vulnerability and preaching the "grace, not perfection" message, because it is so needed for every single one of us.

It has been refreshing to witness to watch it provide hope to many who believed they were alone in their struggles. With the response this transparency has given to those who are willing to strip themselves and bear their hearts to the world, this movement will only continue to gain momentum.

Being made aware of the struggles of those around us allows us to speak life into them, not wallow in our own isolation, and be consistent in prayer and fellowship with one another.

God does not reveal our weaknesses and show us our fragility so that we become powerless or pitiful. He exposes sickness so that we can be healed. He brings brokenness to the light so that we can be restored. He calls shame to the surface so that freedom can be our expression.

Vulnerability is possible because of the hope we have and the promises we know. After we learn to cry together, let us focus on healing together, going to war on one another's behalf, and assuming the authority that we have in the name of Jesus.

Dear Jesus, thank You for giving us the courage and the strength to show up and be vulnerable with others. Help us to remember that You expose weakness so it can be made stronger. We are powerful in Your name, and we choose redemption over pity. In Jesus's name, amen.

A Steellike Hope

But this I call to mind, and therefore I have hope:
The steadfast love of the LORD never ceases;
his mercies never come to an end; they are new
every morning; great is your faithfulness.
LAMENTATIONS 3:21–23 ESV

We have experienced it before—when we get to know someone and witness the fruit of their life in action. We know the hardship they have faced or the impossible circumstances they have come against, and yet their attitude remains consistently joyful. From the outside in, their hope seems inconsistent with their circumstances.

Despite the news from their doctor, the family events they have going on, or the financial struggles they are sorting through, our friends seem okay. The rockiness of their situation has not made them second-guess the goodness of their heavenly Father. Despite their weaknesses, their strength is unshakable. How is this so?

Their hope does not reside here. They have come to realize that it is not the material things, the reputation they hold, the pushing of their own image forward, or the security of a bank account that provides true hope. Hope that can be destroyed or taken away is no hope at all. But eternal hope? It can be tested but not destroyed. It can be questioned but not taken away. It rests in the promises of God.

Where do we place our hope? Do our attitude and perspective change upon the first glance of difficulty? How do we steward our resources? Do we trust that the trials are preparing for us an eternal glory that far outweighs them all?

The depth of our faith and the placement of our hope will always be revealed through the trials and transitions of life. Our hope is not here on this earth. Therefore, disappointments do not have to shatter our soul—and even on our coldest day, we have the warmth of His presence.

Living in our hope is the most powerful sermon we could ever give. It is the decision to believe God, to trust Him with our future, and to walk forward, fully confident that He is at work. A steellike hope... that is what He wants for us.

Dear Jesus, thank You for the gift of hope. No matter where we are or what we face, the assurance of Your provision and love will guide us forward. May our countenance, perspective, and posture reflect our hope in You. You are faithful in all that You do. In Jesus's name, amen.

Expectations from the Garden

This God—his way is perfect;
the word of the LORD proves true;
he is a shield for all those
who take refuge in him.
II SAMUEL 22:31 ESV

The Garden of Eden was a picture of true perfection. All was right with the world. Healing was not necessary because pain was not present. Disappointment was not possible because sin had not entered the scene. Adam and his bride, Eve, were in perfect unity under a perfect God, naked and pure and shameless without a worry in the world. (Really! There was no worry in the world!) Out of Eden came all humanity, and therefore, this picture of perfection in the garden can be found deep within our own heart.

This utopia, which seems like a pipe dream, is still the standard we seek to attain in our own life here on earth. It is out of this place that we create our impossible standards, hoping to achieve perfection as it was back then. But we live in a broken world now, which makes this standard impossible to achieve. Understanding this complexity of our desires and the discrepancies it creates in our mind and in our relationships helps us craft more realistic expectations.

If we want to invest and believe in a hope that does not disappoint, we will have to remember that perfection is only possible in one person: Jesus. This truth is so important to remember, not in providing a scapegoat for our mistakes but in helping us give grace to ourselves and those around us. If we place our hope in people while aligning with our expectations from the garden, we will remain discontent, disappointed, and discouraged. Our hope can only be placed in Jesus—He is the One who can meet our standards, never put us to shame, and will continue to show up every step of the way.

When we find our heart growing weary, let's retrace where we placed our hope. As we learn to continually renew our mind and put our life back in His hands, our soul will cultivate a place of rest. That peace that Adam and Eve felt in the garden? That freedom to be themselves and not hide? It is still ours in Jesus.

Dear Jesus, thank You for making us in Your image, bearing perfection and honor. Will You help us as we craft our own expectations on earth? Help us rely on You and give grace to others. Thank You for loving us. In Jesus's name, amen.

Prayer Paves the Way

Therefore I tell you, whatever you ask for in prayer,
believe that you have received it, and it will be yours.
MARK 11:24 NIV

Remember the game at the arcade where players drop a claw into a big glass bin of stuffed animals and try to grab one of them?

Once in a while, the claw will actually pick up and deliver a fluffy animal that has had its eye poked a few times. But more often than not, the claw will attempt to grab a prize that is too small to remain in the claw or one that holds on for dear life until the drop-off point and yet tragically fails to make it all the way home.

Sometimes we view prayer this way. We deposit quarters and invest but do not expect to yield results. Although prayer was never intended to be a piggy bank, why would we spend our time in conversation with someone who, we feel, doesn't hear us?

But prayer, for so many, many reasons, is vital to our spiritual life. The Bible tells us time and time again that the Lord hears the prayers of His people. He tells us to pray without ceasing (I Thessalonians

5:17 NASB), to pray when we are tempted (Matthew 26:41), to be devoted to prayer (Colossians 4:2 NIV), and many more instances. Prayer is our continual acknowledgment of who is in control and our intentional surrender to His will.

When we devote ourselves to prayer, we open the lines of communication to both being heard and hearing from the One in charge. Prayer is not a loose quarter stuck in a machine that may or may not secure a victory. It is a direct link to the Father; it is immediately deposited, fully heard, and mightily effective. No matter how intricate and small or how cumbersome and heavy something is, He hears our requests.

Prayer invites stillness. It recalibrates our focus. It reminds us of our eternal home. It acknowledges the holiness of God and keeps us humble in our view of ourselves.

Prayer paves the way for miracles, breakthrough, trust, hope, and obedience to be possible. It reminds our soul that our God is greater and He is near.

Dear Jesus, thank You for the opportunity to be in constant conversation with You. Help us to seek Your guidance and wisdom before all else. The good and the bad—everything we are and do— are important to You. Thank You for listening to us and being intimately wired to every heart You created. In Jesus's name, amen.

Remove the Scarlet Letter

But the Lord GOD helps me;
therefore I have not been disgraced;
therefore I have set my face like a flint,
and I know that I shall not be put to shame.
ISAIAH 50:7 ESV

There is messy stuff in our past. Hard stuff. Broken places and stories that we don't really prefer to share. Our history has heartbreak and confusion, lots of fear and mistakes, and a whole lot of us not believing what the good Lord has said about us. If we go back there? It feels too heavy. Doesn't He want us to live in the present? We tell ourselves this, being afraid to look in the rearview mirror and see the person we once were in case we still look anything like them.

But who said our past has to be labeled "toxic" simply because it is uncomfortable? That's not to say that it is healthy to rehearse strongholds and past fears or marinate on what used to be. However, we would be foolish to not glean from our past and realize that Jesus made no mistakes about how we got to where we are today. Our past was never supposed to be our source of shame but rather our springboard to something so much greater.

When we "scarlet letter" ourselves and let guilt or shame be the label we place on our past, we strip them of the power they provide in our present. When we say we believe in the redemptive power of Jesus, we are stating in full confidence that we know our past has prepared our heart for this present moment. Our capability, compassion, and calling have been made possible by both our mistakes and our successes. Because we know the depth of our pit, we more greatly comprehend the strength and magnitude of the grace required to take us to where we are today.

The Lord is wildly attracted to our weakness. Masking the pain of past experiences keeps us and others from witnessing mercy in motion. We are where we are for such a time as this, with such a story as this, for such a purpose as this. Our old selves have prepared us for our future plans, and we have been made new.

Dear Jesus, thank You for taking all our guilt and our shame upon the cross. We know that Your redemptive power turns even our biggest failures into springboards for greatness. You make all things good and glorious. Help us to see our past with a hopeful heart. In Jesus's name, Amen.

Stillness Invites the Prompting

When the Spirit of truth comes,
he will guide you into all the truth,
for he will not speak on his own authority,
but whatever he hears he will speak,
and he will declare to you the things that are to come.
JOHN 16:13 ESV

Remember as a child when bedtime was way earlier than desired and no one thought they were tired—until they were forced to get horizontal and everyone went out like a light? Or when quiet time was encouraged at church camp and everyone was silently doubting their ability to journal what they were hearing from God until the quiet surrounded them? Then all around the place, pens were going a million miles per hour, scribbling what God was depositing into the heart.

Both of these examples show us that oftentimes, until something is forced upon us, we do not realize how much it was calling our name. Stillness is the same way. We believe our laborious tasks offer a far more productive outcome than stillness could ever provide and so we dodge it like a bullet. Or we dodge our own ability to hear God speak, and so we never give Him the invitation to do so.

But just like a child when bedtime hits or a quiet time that forces us to slow down, creating a time of stillness invites the prompting for whatever needs to happen, to happen. How do we expect to hear from God when we have given Him no time to speak or read the words He has already written to us? He is not silent, and we are not deaf. It is that He is not forceful and we are not intentional.

When we allow for this time, we give space for the Holy Spirit to do what He was designed to do inside of us. Clarity is brought to the surface. Decisions go from gray to black-and-white as remembrance of His instruction comes to our mind. Comfort becomes a close friend as we draw close to Jesus.

We often have no idea of what we need and far too much of an idea of what we want. But when we are still, we are reminded that He is all we need and the only One who knows what we truly desire.

Dear Jesus, thank You for the way You faithfully show up when we make time for You. Help us to create this time of stillness and allow our spirit to be prompted, giving us direction for the steps ahead and the decisions to come. In Jesus's name, amen.

"*Yes, my soul,
find rest in God;
my hope
comes from Him.*"

PSALM 62:5 NIV

Living on Autopilot

Look carefully then how you walk,
not as unwise but as wise,
making the best use of the time,
because the days are evil.
EPHESIANS 5:15–16 ESV

We have all had the experience of driving somewhere, arriving, and having absolutely no idea how we got there safely. We went through stoplights, made a few turns, and shifted gears, all without really telling our brain to do anything. The autopilot kicked into gear.

How often do we operate like this in other parts of our life? We establish thought patterns and drive down the same "roads"—and before we know it, they become our go-to routes. We see the results they cause and we want our life to look differently, but we also want the new thought patterns to come easily. The work feels too hard; shouldn't it come easier if the desire is there? We forget the power of autopilot and the tendency to jump into our car, turn on the music, and drive without intentionally deciding where we are going.

We wonder why our hope feels drained, but we

have not chosen a new method of thinking.

We are frustrated with the lack of progress on our dreams, but we have made no efforts to carve out time to work on them.

We yearn for self-confidence, yet we rehearse the same lies over ourselves and our body. We have to do some rewiring. The Lord is really good at giving our brain new truths to marinate on and our soul new promises to hope in, but we must spend time with Him first.

Being still with Jesus is the only way to reverse our autopilot lifestyle and create a more intentional route.

We do not have to clean up or pretend as though we have been intentionally aware; He knows when we are just moving through life. We do not have to wait until we get to another corner in order for Him to get involved—we can begin now. Even though we will want to turn on the music when we feel like life is asking too much of us, if we can just lean into Him and be still as He leads, we will experience the fullest life possible.

No more autopilot; life is too short and too grand to waste on simply existing.

Dear Jesus, thank You for the way that You lead us, even when our pride or fear has kept us from seeking You. Show us the way to go. Turn off the music, shut off our distractions, remove "autopilot" mode, and let us be alert as we seek Your will. In Jesus's name, amen.

When God Is Silent in Our Stillness

Blessed are those who hunger and thirst for righteousness,
for they shall be satisfied.
MATTHEW 5:6 ESV

We've all had the experience where we have consulted with God on a situation or a relationship in our life and felt like we could not hear Him speaking about it. Our frustration grew as we wanted to remind Him that He was the One who asked us to draw near—but He was quiet...why? What were we supposed to do? The prayers of our heart felt pressing and urgent, and it seemed as if the Lord had taken a vacation.

We must always know that the Lord is not quiet seemingly because He does not know the answers. The depth of our depravity or the uncertainty of our circumstances has not forced Him to retreat. Sometimes the Lord does not answer via burning bush because His Word has already answered the question for us. Have we searched the Bible to inform our heart of the truth regarding our situation? Or have we only let our emotions dictate what is coming out of our mouth?

Other times, the Lord is silent because He is silent. He is God. Despite our human desire to receive an explanation for unfilled airwaves, He does not answer to us. His silence does not license us to run and seek a louder voice; His silence is our invitation to draw deeper into stillness. When we grasp the truth that God is God and sometimes our life will feel full of the unknown, we can begin to walk in peace that stretches beyond our understanding. Where we mess up is when we equate His silence as His absence. He is always working.

When we feel like God is silent, we must continue to seek. As we seek and discover truth, this truth invites true transformation. His silence is not His dismissal of our voice; it is His desire for us to keep coming, keep pursuing, keep searching for His wisdom amid our uncertainty. We become His image bearers as we pursue His voice in the quiet.

The resting of our hope cannot be found in our solutions. Our heart is anchored in the King of kings who never leaves the authority and power of His throne.

Dear Jesus, thank You for always answering in the most perfect way, even when that feels like absence to us. Remind us to continue pursuing You and disciplining ourselves in stillness. Your silence is an invitation, not a dismissal. You are God alone, and we trust Your ways. In Jesus's name, amen.

Discovering Our Purpose

Many are the plans in a person's heart,
but it is the LORD's purpose that prevails.
PROVERBS 19:21 NIV

Purpose...it's one of those popular terms in today's culture, but if you ask everyone for their definition of the word, it is about as elusive as the Loch Ness Monster. And in our hurried culture? It is usually defined by what we can see.

What do our hands do? How are our days spent? We often believe this is proof of whether or not we are pursuing our purpose. While what we do matters, the Lord's greatest concern is with who we are becoming. Therein lies our true purpose and mission: looking like Jesus.

In general terms, our purpose is to show the love of our heavenly Father to every human soul we encounter so that they may more intimately know Him and long to be with Him too. This cannot happen through words or deeds alone but in becoming more like Jesus. When we begin to resemble our heavenly Father, our heart is infectious, our spirit is magnetic, and our life is like a sunbeam. The King of kings and Almighty God does not need our assistance because it is too much for Him; rather, He allows us to partner with Him so that our life can mean something...so that we can taste true purpose, eternal purpose, a purpose that extends far beyond ourselves and lasts in the next lifetime.

Seeking stillness and adjusting to the rhythm of our God allows us to rightfully define our purpose, looking inwardly to evaluate and test our heart rather than let our life be a performance of what our hands do. When walking in step with Jesus, we can hear Him as He instructs, "A little to the right...there you go" and finding that balance is no longer on our own terms.

Lord, thank You that You desire to mold us, transform us, and use us according to Your purposes. Renew our mind when we begin to define our worth by what our hands are doing, and recalibrate us to the truth. Thank You for giving us opportunities to serve You and look more like You. In Jesus's name, amen.

What's Your Name Again?

*Having purified your souls by your obedience
to the truth for a sincere brotherly love,
love one another earnestly from a pure heart.*
I PETER 1:22 ESV

Remembering other people's names is pivotal in making them feel heard and significant. We often underestimate the value in remembering the names of those we meet, thanks to our inability to listen carefully or convincing ourselves that we can just find them on social media. The whole "kinda sorta" listening disorder in full effect.

A question to consider: did we ever see Jesus having trouble remembering the names of those He was around or serving? Names were important to Him. While it seems like such a simple act, this is one of the easiest ways we have at our disposal to let others know they are not overlooked or undervalued.

Being still and opening up our heart to Jesus does not just keep us from becoming crazy people; it reveals to our heart those in our path that need to be loved. It helps us look more deeply into their life. It provides us with the time and space to ask the hard questions and to truly stick around to hear their answers.

We cannot ask God to show us who and where to serve and then explain to Him why we have no time, mental capacity, or emotional bandwidth left to go where He instructs or love who He commands.

It is also true that when we give our soul time to breathe, it works to our benefit in every capacity. We are sharper in our ability to distinguish between right and wrong. We are obedient in our seeking out of others, generous with our time, and confident that the Lord is guiding our steps. We become better about seeing others as Jesus does—no longer as interruptions or inconveniences but rather as beloved, capable, and significant.

Lord, thank You for helping us to be still in You so that we can greater understand how to love those around us. Give us eyes to see their needs, willing hands to help them, and an obedient spirit that does not question the appointments You put in our paths. Thank You for loving us so well so that we may pour out some of that love onto those around us. In Jesus's name, amen.

An Identity Issue

*But you are a chosen people,
a royal priesthood, a holy nation,
God's special possession,
that you may declare the praises of Him
who called you out of darkness
into His wonderful light.*

I PETER 2:9 NIV

Why is stillness so difficult? Why do we feel the need to be everything to everyone and everywhere all the time? Do we truly desire this type of demanding lifestyle, or have these expectations been placed on us because we have forgotten who we are?

If we think about it, the only reason we would add a million things to our to-do list and try to please everyone around us is because we desire their approval. The only reason we would be attempting to secure their validation is because we have forgotten our inherent value as children of the Most High King. This lack of belief in ourselves puts our security out in the open, waiting and vulnerable for anyone to discredit, disapprove, or deem us unworthy.

When we take the time to dig into Scripture and study what the Lord thinks about us, we learn that God says we're deeply loved, wonderfully made, and part of His master plan. Our rushed approach to life makes us forget who we are and the price that has already been spoken over our life. We cheapen our worth because we are too tired to fight for it.

But we were never supposed to fight to attain our identity—the Lord has already gone before us, knows our shortcomings, and carried the cross up the hill anyway. Our level of "worthy" has never been up for question; it has always been our belief that is in question. When we allow our mind and body to be still, we allow our soul to hear what our Maker says about us. The lies become glaringly obvious and our awareness is increased—"I know who I am; that is not of Jesus"—we now can detect it, reject it, and replace it with truth. Knowing our true identity is the key to living a life of purpose.

Dear Jesus, thank You for weaving us perfectly in Your image. When we find our mind wandering or letting our identity be up for negotiation, take us back to Your Word and the truth that sets us free. In Jesus's name, amen.

Long Story Short, Please

God did this so that they would seek Him
and perhaps reach out for Him and find Him,
though He is not far from any one of us.
ACTS 17:27 NIV

Have you ever noticed how we never want to have to hear the whole story? We much prefer the abridged version, with the meat of the story, the climax, and the conclusion all meshed into one, requiring very little to no brain power to comprehend.

While this version may be our preference when zooming through a less-than-exhilarating novel, this mode of intake is killing our faith. We have unlimited podcasts at our fingertips, 24-hour news cycles, downloadable songs and movies with the click of a button, and there is only more to come in the future. This ability to have information immediately has made us wildly impatient and uncomfortable with having to search out truth for ourselves.

Instead of spending time connecting with God, we cram ourselves full of information. And this is certainly not to say that all these things are not incredibly enlightening, important, and innovative. Our world and the technology age has made becoming a student of any topic relatively affordable, and it is amazing. However, there is no replacement for time spent learning the heart of our heavenly Father.

We can gain knowledge of who He is and what He commands from our life, but until we spend time being with Him, worshipping Him, and showing up to receive love from Him, we will forever wonder how to apply this knowledge.

The long story short is, well, there is no long story short. Increasing our faith requires our diligence and our stillness. Gaining a hopeful heart is not achieved by mere acquisition of knowledge; it is possible through the grace and love when leaning into the arms of our heavenly Father. No abridged version, no outline, no bulleted list—just a relationship formed through His tender touch and teaching.

Jesus, thank You that You desire to know each of us intimately and personally. While learning about You builds knowledge, connecting to You produces peace. Help us seek You, desire more of You, and make being with You a necessary part of our everyday life. In Jesus's name, amen.

Letting the Dirt Fall

The unfolding of your words gives light;
it imparts understanding to the simple.
PSALM 119:130 ESV

Mindfulness is a trendy subject right now, which makes sense considering how difficult it is to get alone with our thoughts in the hectic culture that surrounds us.

We use an application on our phone to remind us to be still, but the application gets interrupted by a call or a text beckoning our attention. As we pick up our phone to react to the prompted communication, our schedule already gets off-kilter. As people knock and unexpected circumstances arise, the distinction between "important" and "urgent" gets murky and we feel oh so defeated.

"Lord, can You just show us what You want us to do?"—isn't that how we feel?

Think about this for a moment: for a glass of dirty water to become clean, set it on a counter. Unmoved. When it seems to have rested, let it rest a little more. Even when we believe the purified water is completely clear at the top, there is still some dirt that will eventually fall to the bottom if the glass sits still long enough.

This purification process is so similar to that of our own heart and mind. We search for clarity and strength and direction, but all the while, we are trying to see through dirty water! Seeing requires patience and stillness. Letting the dirt fall is a discipline, because to be honest, we can often get by with the mediocre. We have delivered and nurtured that hazy filter for so long that it has become our normal.

But something miraculous happens when we let Jesus work in us and through us and we fight for the crystal-clear view. When we sit and then sit some more, we allow our mind to really grasp what the Lord says about us and who we are because of who He is! We begin to quickly recognize what is important and what is urgent, and we no longer simply react to the events of our days. The water of our life becomes purified through the filter of His truth and the light it brings. Sit still and let the dirt fall. He is doing a mighty work.

Jesus, thank You for the invitation You give us to sit and be still with You. Help us prioritize this, remembering that all else in our life will sort itself out when we give You our focus. Thank You for showing us what is urgent and what is important. In Jesus's name, amen.

Loving Like Jesus Does

*This is my commandment, that you love one another as
I have loved you. Greater love has no one than this, that
someone lay down his life for his friends. You are my
friends if you do what I command you.*

JOHN 15:12-14 ESV

How often do we find ourselves switching from loving
to bothered/frustrated/bitter/angry because we
feel the need to reciprocate? We hear about loving
unconditionally, but our human heart is so used to
loving based on emotion and changing circumstances
that it is hard to fathom a love unwavering.

But what if we made it our mission? Instead
of getting even, we could commit our heart to
forgiveness and offering a true clean slate to another?
What if, when we feel slighted or excluded from a
situation, we do not hold tight to bitterness or fear
and still offer our love freely?

What if it stopped being about everything we
receive and became about what we can give—
regardless of the response, the rejection, the lack
of reciprocation, or reassurance? It would confuse

others and lead them right to this thought: "Why do they give love that I have not deserved?" Herein lies the perfect opportunity for our heart to exclaim, "Jesus!" His eternal hope is the reason we can love so freely in return, knowing that He will work as He sees fit.

Wouldn't that be incredible? To not be scared to be the people who love more, forgive freely, give grace abundantly, and walk in a confidence that stems from the ever-flowing love of Jesus? That would be the gospel.

Our heart is fragile. We take things personally. We are scared to let in others once we've been wronged. We have been taught by the world to only give what we receive—they must be worthy.

But Jesus calls us to love others out of a heart that is fully and recklessly loved by Him. This does not mean our emotions become absent and our pain won't be felt; it just means that when those things do happen, we can remind ourselves we're already accepted and abundantly loved by our Creator. It is in this truth that we no longer crave and depend on the reassurance of this world, and we begin to look like people of hope.

Dear Jesus, thank You for loving us beyond what we can ever fathom or deserve. You are so gracious to us. Remind our heart to not take things personally and to love others the way You love us. In Jesus's name, amen.

Practice Pausing

The Lord is good to those who wait for him,
to the soul who seeks him.
LAMENTATIONS 3:25 ESV

The Apple watch is pretty neat. It takes into account many different factors throughout the day and offers insight into our personal rhythms. I have found it extremely informative in showing my habits and tendencies.

The discovery of my own personal rhythm forced me to change some things. I was going to sleep way too late and not getting my heart rate up first thing in the morning—and everything else was being affected. Making these changes initiated several other habits, as once I began getting more rest and getting my workout completed first thing in the morning, the rest of my day offered different opportunities. My Apple watch also allows me to set different alarms, including reminders to breathe and slow down. While it seems unnecessary, these often come at the perfect time and have made me realize how little I used to pause.

Pausing is much the same for all of us. Is there

ever an opportune time to slow down when we have so much to do? It feels counterintuitive and unproductive. Childish, even. But much like the habit of going to sleep earlier, carving out time for intentional solitude affects every other part of our day.

Meetings will pop up, e-mails will need to be sent, children will be sick from school, and opportunities to avoid pausing will always present themselves. But much like any other habit or desired change in our life, the more we practice something, the better we get at it. The more we see the results of a particular discipline, the easier it becomes to require it of ourselves. The further we get away from where we once were with a particular habit, the clearer it becomes that change was, in fact, necessary.

How can we practice pausing in life today? Are we afraid of what the Lord might reveal when we stop long enough to hear Him?

Let's let our heart slip into that restful state—pausing and remembering to be grateful, collecting our emotions and resuming our posture of peace, and choosing a different rhythm for our life.

Eventually we will not even need the alarm to go off! How exciting will that be?

Dear Jesus, thank You for being present at all times. Today, we choose to pause and notice Your presence and provision. When we get frustrated with our wandering mind, give us grace to extend to ourselves. Help us pause. In Jesus's name, amen.

No Time for Resentment

Fear not, for you will not be put to shame;
and do not feel humiliated,
for you will not be disgraced;
but you will forget the shame of your youth,
and the reproach of your widowhood
you will remember no more.

ISAIAH 54:4 NASB

We should be used to it. It is not a new trick or an impressive switch of strategy. Isn't this what happens every time we begin to ignite change in our life or seek to form a new perspective? As soon as we turn a corner, set new goals, or establish a fresh mind-set, it starts to feel as if we're being sabotaged from every angle. Whether it is new frustrations, unforeseen life events, or shameful feelings from our past life, something starts to stand in our way—causing us to give up on our efforts for change.

And while we know it is not good for us, sometimes choosing to live in what should have been is easier than dealing with the present. It is more comfortable to hold onto what's hurt us, to make others pay for the wrongs they've extended to us, or to remain in our shame and our own self-resentment for the mistakes we've made. We give into temptation, letting it become a pattern, and before we realize it, we've let our present be compromised by the mistakes of our past.

But we have a greater hope. We have no time for resentment because we are too busy singing praises to God. Our eyes have a light in them because we are children of the Most High God; we have places to go and people to reach.

As we approach our day today, let us throw off everything that entangles us. We are chosen and equipped—may we see ourselves as so.

Dear Jesus, thank You for offering us a clean slate with every day that passes. Your grace really is more than enough. Help us let go of any resentment we hold against ourselves or others. Thank You for the opportunity to run confidently in You. In Jesus's name, amen.

*"The first act
of love is
always the giving
of attention."*

DALLAS WILLARD

Don't Borrow from Tomorrow

Therefore do not worry about tomorrow,
for tomorrow will worry about itself.
Each day has enough trouble of its own.
MATTHEW 6:34 NIV

There it goes again. We keep reaching for it. Our hands are full of today's responsibilities and yet we strain to try to reach into the jar of tomorrow. "What's in there?" we wonder. "Can I handle it?" we ponder.

We presume, do our best to predict, and conclude accordingly. We begin toiling, rocking back and forth, trying to make a plan, gathering treasures and hoping they'll be enough—all based on our best guess at what the future could possibly hold.

When the Lord told us that His grace is sufficient for our weakness, He meant within the confines of one day. He instructed us to remain in the present because our ability to remain hopeful when we begin assuming and assessing is minuscule. We have no concept of how God will connect the dots or how life will transform by the time tomorrow actually arrives.

When we dig into tomorrow, we borrow grief

and concern that was never meant for us to carry. The forecast for a day we have never experienced will always seem more daunting—"How will I have the money/time/energy to do that?" "Will I feel this alone?" "Has God forgotten about this?" All these questions plague our mind and invite us to snowball into the roller coaster of tomorrow.

This is the reality—grief will knock. So will disappointment. Rejection will have its day. Hardship will be a guest at our table. But when they show up, we will be ready! The Lord will have prepared us for such a time, and He will sustain us with each passing day. Reaching into tomorrow's jar is the decision not to embrace what is being offered to us today.

As we discipline ourselves in staying in today's time frame, we will realize how lightly we travel. It no longer requires a million bags and a mapped-out plan to experience victory; it simply requires trusting Jesus for today and not borrowing from tomorrow.

Dear Jesus, thank You for reminding us to remember the gift of today. We know nothing of tomorrow, but You do, and You will go before us. Help us to travel lightly. Tomorrow will come, and when it does, You will have prepared us to conquer it. In Jesus's name, amen.

Kingdom Builders

For God has not given us a spirit of fear,
but of power and of love and of a sound mind.
II TIMOTHY 1:7 NKJV

How often do we give energy to thoughts that deserve none of our attention? We play the "what-if" game, entertaining any and all possibilities of the future. Our imagination gets the best of us, and we forget to filter those thoughts through the truth.

How frequently does our situation turn out exactly as we assumed it would? More often than not, so many of our predicted outcomes never come to fruition, and we are mentally worn out by the unnecessary roller coaster. We imagine how the puzzle pieces will all fit together, and then the Lord blows our mind. Somehow, someway, the resources are provided, the tangible details come together, and all ends up being okay.

No matter where we are or what we have on our plate, if we continue to rehearse fear, we will miss out on operating in the faith He has instilled in us. The reason it is called a "leap of faith" is because there is a little air in between those steps, a little uncertainty in between those stones. It requires us getting out of our own head and trusting fully in Him. It requires us remembering that while our paralysis feels permanent, we know it is not—we know we must silence the chatter in our head and trust the One who calms our heart.

If we think for a moment that those who are shakers and doers, big dreamers, and serious kingdom-builders operate without fear, then we are seriously mistaken. They just have decided that the world is big and full of life and they serve the Creator of it! They have decided that if they want to experience the view, they will have to overcome their fear of heights.

Because when they do? When we do? When we get out of ourselves and stop rehearsing our fears, our mind follows suit. We are capable of far more than we realize. We are eternity shapers who step forward in courage and have the power of a sound mind.

Dear Jesus, thank You for the reminder to focus on You and not rehearse the future based on circumstances and details we do not know. Help us trust You, taking one step at a time, believing You to provide when necessary. In Jesus's name, amen.

Stop Freaking Out

We demolish arguments and every pretension
that sets itself up against the knowledge of God,
and we take captive every thought
to make it obedient to Christ.

II CORINTHIANS 10:5 NIV

Beth Moore made this brilliant statement: "You can go ahead and freak out, or you might just choose to believe that God is going to be faithful."

It is brilliant because every single one of us can relate. And if we are being honest, we often choose the first option of freaking out, don't we? Something goes awry and we are in a tailspin before we even understand what it all means. We jump to conclusions, assume the worst, allow irrational thoughts to cloud our judgment, and let our emotions tell us what's next.

When we freak out, we miss so much that is right in front of our eyes. It's like we take on tunnel vision, only permitting our memory to retain the negative. We forget, in just one situation, what the Lord has already done for us. Is that all it took—something going wrong—for us to assume that He is not in control and we need to put matters into our own hands? Our "plans" were interrupted, and instead of viewing this as an opportunity for God to do His thing, we question whether God is even present.

Believe it or not, we always have a choice. Even in the stickiest situations or when our backs are so hard-pressed against a wall that we can't see anything else, we can still choose to trust God.

Will it make sense in our little box of normality or comfort? Will it be easy? Will it fix itself immediately? Probably not, to all these.

But aren't these the very moments we were created for? To be warriors of faith? To pick the side of trust and stay on the battlefield? He has never failed us. Ever. He does not lead us into traps; He guides us in His truth. His promises are secure.

So let's chill a little bit. And when we want to freak out, vent, or worry, let's reel it in. Let's remind ourselves of who we serve and remember His track record: He is always faithful.

Dear Jesus, thank You for being a calming Father. When we feel ourselves getting overwhelmed, can You remind us of Your faithfulness? Reserve our energy for what matters and give us the wisdom to consult You first and foremost. In Jesus's name, amen.

Show Me the Chains

For freedom Christ has set us free;
stand firm therefore, and do not submit again
to a yoke of slavery.
GALATIANS 5:1 ESV

Even in our very best, all of us have things that are holding us back from experiencing the best God has for us.

Sometimes that can be an inherently bad thing, like an addiction or an affair, choices of separation from God that we know are restricting our ability to walk freely in Him.

Other times, our entanglements look like the roses in our life. There is nothing wrong with the resources, hobbies, or relationships we have, but due to our stewardship of them, they have become idols. What the Lord desired for our good can quickly be used against us if we are not aware, prioritizing Him first and foremost.

We all have our kryptonite, and while we know it is hurting us, we still crave its existence or the outcome it brings. We fear who we will be without the substance. We worry that we will lose the possibility of a promotion if we work any less. We concern ourselves with meticulous details of our appearance.

These things in our life become chains, and they prevent us from pursuing our calling. Our fulfillment becomes compromised by our comfort because our comfort has become our kryptonite. We fear what life would look like without our crutch, and we deceive ourselves into thinking all is okay. We can manage, right?

This crutch steals our joy and works hard to make us forget our identity in Christ. We were created to live courageously. To live freely. To do the hard things and look differently than the world. We were not designed to hang out in the mediocre places, because our God has an abundant life in store for us.

Let's let Him reveal our chains—however they look—and be willing to take them off. Surrender will require transparency of our struggles, awareness of God's promises for our life, patience with ourselves, and fervent fortitude as we take a step into freedom. He is near and He is working. Let us run with the wind at our back and our eyes on Jesus.

Dear Jesus, thank You for making us free. There is nothing we must do to loosen our chains except fully trust in You. Show us our limitations; break off our fears. Lead us in Your righteousness. In Jesus's name, amen.

Divinely Placed and Purposed

For if you remain silent at this time,
relief and deliverance for the Jews will arise from another
place, but you and your father's family will perish.
And who knows but that you have come
to your royal position for such a time as this?
ESTHER 4:14 NIV

Remember the Bible story about Jesus using an ordinary boy carrying five loaves of bread and two fish to produce a meal for a crowd of five thousand?

Or what about when Esther was chosen to be queen of Persia, in turn saving the entire Jewish population?

Or what about Joseph, who, after being rejected by his brothers, was made king of Egypt and saves their lives?

Each of these stories represents a common thread that is woven into the fabric of our own testimonies: we have been divinely placed "for such a time as this" (Esther 4:14 NIV). Sometimes life is weird and confusing. Circumstances are less than preferred and we are just not where we thought we would be. But what if our perspective changed?

What if we started believing in this moment that God is big enough and mighty enough to get us to where He wants us to go? What if, instead of planning and worrying and desperately trying to make sense of what isn't, you focused on all that is?

We follow Jesus. He is the miracle worker, and His desire for our life is not only to use us, but that we would do even greater works than He did on earth (John 14:12). The mundane is often the exact preparation we need for the miracle in our own backyard. But if we are trying so hard to get to somewhere else rather than walking in our purpose exactly where we are today, we might miss our opportunity.

We have an on-time God who is never a second off in His delivery. He has not forgotten our desires. What feels like denial is often His delay, allowing our heart to be refined and ready for the blessing. Divinely placed and purposed, that is our assurance.

Dear Jesus, thank You for positioning us exactly where You want us to be. We know that Your best for our life is far greater than our mind can comprehend. Make us aware of our purpose where we are and help us to do Your will. In Jesus's name, amen.

Intentional White Space

Teach us to number our days,
that we may gain a heart of wisdom.
PSALM 90:12 NIV

How often do we get to the end of the day and realize that it's the first time all day we have taken a deep breath? We sit down to take off our makeup or lay horizontally in bed and think, "Well, that was a whirlwind."

Part of us likes this feeling, this blow-through-the-day, I'm-so-busy type of feeling, because we equate it with significance. We are needed. Wanted where we are. Important to the causes we support, the office we go to, the family we serve, or wherever we spend our hours. But secretly, we wish we had margin. We need it.

However, when we do have margin or the opportunity for a moment alone, we start doing something *stat*. If not, we are wasteful, right? Or that's how we have deemed it.

It's this weird phenomenon that we have grown to hate yet refuse to abandon. We wish the world didn't travel at one hundred miles per hour and determine our value based on our accolades, but why would the world define us differently than we do ourselves?

The myth is that white space is for those who are lazy or lack purpose. But the truth is that white space is for those who are diligent and seek purpose. Carving out margin in the confines of our day is not just suggested, it is necessary! When we allow ourselves to *be* for a moment, without feeling the need to document it, we are forced to reconcile the story for ourselves.

Do we allow our commitments and schedule to define our identity? Or does our identity determine our commitments and schedule? Let's find some time today for white space, even if that means declining a lunch date or trimming a bullet off our to-do list. In order to bring our best selves along, we need to have the space to discover just who that person is.

We do not need a calendar to confirm our value. We need white space so that we can spend time with our Father, the Giver of all our significance.

Dear Jesus, remind me that white space is okay. It does not mean I am unimportant; it means I am intentional. Thank You for reminding our soul that our significance is not based on our schedule. Our most valuable time is spent with You. Give us a heart of wisdom so that we may be intentional with our time and our life. In Jesus's name, amen.

Where Faith and Hope Reside

*And now I want each of you to extend
that same intensity toward a full-bodied hope,
and keep at it till the finish. Don't drag your feet.
Be like those who stay the course with committed faith
and then get everything promised to them.*
HEBREWS 6:11–12 THE MESSAGE

What is the difference between faith and hope? Faith is "the assurance of things hoped for, the conviction of things not seen" (Hebrews 11:1 ESV), and hope is defined as that same assuredness but in the future (Hebrews 6:9–12 NKJV).

We seem to understand faith as term of certainty, an absolute confidence in the plans, promises, and presence of the Lord. However, we often use the word *hope* with a more wishy-washy meaning than *faith*. We hope the kicker makes the field goal; we hope the restaurant is not crowded; and we hope our presentation goes well—all of which are wishful thinking, not statements of faith. Hope was never meant to be fickle thoughts about our future, able to be washed away with the first wave of opposition.

Hope is ironed-out faith and expressed certainty about a situation, relationship, circumstance, or happening in the future. It operates with full trust that God will show up. The reason why our hope is fickle is because we often place it in the wrong things or the wrong people. Our hope feels vulnerable because when placed in anything but our Creator, it can easily be snatched away. Disappointment can shatter it, insecurity can crush it, and fear can convince it to be silent.

But the hope we have? It is our faith in action. Hope and faith are intertwined, requiring one for the other. Because we have faith in the One who holds our today and our tomorrow, we have hope for our future. And it is the visualizing of our hope that often gives us the strength we need to continue to operate in our faith today. Hope was never meant to be a wish fountain or a genie; it is confident expectation that God will be God.

Faith is confidence that the darkness will lift, and hope continues to dream because it believes that statement of faith to be true. Hopeful hearts are rich in faith *and* hope because they have received the greatest of these—love—from our heavenly Father.

Dear Jesus, thank You for being the Author of our Faith and the Giver of our hope. Our hope is secure in You. Iron out our doubts and challenge our faith so that we may be beacons of hope to a lost world. We trust You with all that we are, wherever we are. In Jesus's name, amen.

Fullness of Joy

You make known to me the path of life;
in your presence there is fullness of joy;
at your right hand are pleasures forevermore.
PSALM 16:11 ESV

Joy often feels elusive, doesn't it? The butterfly we cannot catch, that piece of ribbon blowing in the wind we just cannot seem to grab... We know it's there, so it is certainly real, but it feels impossible to attain. We hear the phrase "choose joy" and it could not feel more out of reach.

Sometimes our situations are so involved and intense that separating ourselves from them feels impossible. In the thick of the trenches, when our feet feel paralyzed in the mud that surrounds us, how do we pretend as though we do not feel stuck? Does God expect us to have joy right then? He can see what life looks like—surely He means *after* we get through this hurdle.

But Scripture tells us that in order to experience joy, there is one necessary ingredient, and that is the presence of Jesus. When we make ourselves sit still in Him and we just "be," our entire being experiences joy. Sometimes it will be like a swift wind, where once we sit down and really step back from everything, joy will come upon us quickly. However, more often than not, this joy will not feel like the joy we experience when attending a theme park or receiving an answer to prayer; it will be more like a stream of water that seeps into all areas of life and purifies our heart.

Our mind is able to lighten its load of worries and to-do lists. Our body is able to relinquish the burdens we have been carrying along our way. Our emotions are able to stabilize as we center ourselves in His arms. We feel renewed as we are reminded who we are and *whose* we are. Our soul does not have the words, because all we can say is "home."

As we relax in His presence, He speaks life back into us and reflects His mirror of identity and then we know we are okay. The realization of our hope and the mere existence of His presence gives us back our joy. It was never gone.

Dear Jesus, thank You for being the Light of our life and the Giver of all joy. Spending time with You and being loved by You reignites our entire being. Help us to remain in this fullness as we rest in You for the remainder of our days. In Jesus's name, amen.

Anticipation versus Anxiety

Do not be anxious about anything,
but in every situation, by prayer and petition,
with thanksgiving, present your requests to God.
And the peace of God, which transcends
all understanding, will guard your hearts
and your minds in Christ Jesus.
PHILIPPIANS 4:6-7 NIV

For some, it is pursuing a dream that has been brewing. For others, it is a move to a new city or church. And for some, it is simply the uncertainty of the future. All these moments present a crossroads where both uncertainty and promise coexist. In each of these moments, we can either become anxious or excitedly anticipate what is next.

We have grown accustomed to treating uncertainty as though it requires anxiety. Because the lights are off, our brain begins to imagine what could be there, and our thoughts get the best of us. But in every moment that we experience anxiety, there is also another path we can let our mind travel down instead: the pathway of anticipation. When we feel out of control and are unsure of what is next, we can take great comfort in the fact that our God is always fighting for our best and preparing the way to get there.

If around the bend lies hardship, it is because the preparation is required for the journey ahead. Let's harness our mind and arrest our anxious thoughts. They hold great power in determining how strongly we plant our feet into the next moment. Let us imagine the ways God is moving on our behalf. Let us dream about the ways we want to serve and grow and speak those into the world. Let us talk with others in a confident manner so that our hope is never in question despite the uncertainty that is up ahead.

Our God is going to show up. That is assured. The rest of the details? They really are somewhat irrelevant. The exact position our feet are in now provide an opportunity to trust God and believe He is who He says He is. Let this be a catalyst to our faith as we get excited about the future! Whatever comes from His hand? It will be good. Anticipate!

Dear Lord, thank You for being a God of provision and for always giving us Your best. We do not fear what is ahead because we know who is in control. Help us choose thoughts that anticipate Your goodness instead of anxious thoughts that doubt it. In Jesus's name, amen.

Increased Demand Requires Stillness

Yet the news about Him spread all the more,
so that crowds of people came to hear Him
and to be healed of their sicknesses.
But Jesus often withdrew
to lonely places and prayed.
LUKE 5:15–16 NIV

Jesus, the Savior of the world and the only Being of perfection, withdrew to lonely places and prayed. Even though He was the Son of God, Jesus never became arrogant in His need for His Father's wisdom.

Luke states that as more crowds of people came to hear Jesus and receive the power of His healing hands, He withdrew to these lonely places more often. Jesus knew that when the demands of His ministry grew, the necessity to spend time in solitude with God was even more crucial.

How often do we lose sight of this example in our own life? We find out we receive a promotion at our workplace, and instead of spending more time reading the Word in the mornings to prepare for this elevated level of obligation, we spend less time in the

Word and get to the office earlier. We will "be still" once the job slows a bit, right?

We increase our level of involvement in the church, and instead of spending time at night thanking Him for our day as we used to, we pass out from sheer exhaustion. We convince ourselves that church is ministry and we will catch up on our personal solitude later, yes?

However our demand looks, when there is an increase in our obligation, platform, or responsibilities in any way, stillness becomes even more important than before. Take an example from Jesus—He knew that the more was asked of Him, the more He would need His own cup refilled. He came humbly to His Father, fully dependent upon His strength.

But He had to withdraw. He knew that in order to hear His Father, He needed to be alone. This required being intentional with going to these lonely places wherever He was and seeking Him. May we do the same, wherever we are, and reframe our mind to believe that stillness is required in order to be effective.

Dear Jesus, thank You for being a true example of a servant. Amid all, You always chose time with God. Help us to prioritize solitude with You, especially when stillness feels difficult to attain. We want to seek You and hear Your voice. Refill our cup. In Jesus's name, amen.

"Our adversary majors in three things: noise, hurry, and crowds. If he can keep us engaged in 'muchness' and 'manyness,' he will rest satisfied."

RICHARD J. FOSTER

Being in Awe

Be still,
and know that I am God.
PSALM 46:10 NIV

We often read and interpret stillness to reference rest. We assume the viewpoint of stillness as inactivity; therefore, all movement is stopped. Because of the world we live in, with constant deadlines and the cultural rat race, this becomes our invitation to rest.

And while it does mean "rest" in one sense, the Lord commands us to "be still." He is emphatic. His words in Psalm 46:10 direct us to be still, not asleep. This stillness is not one of laziness but rather a directive to cease striving and moving and gaining and running—to be still in the presence of God.

God is not telling us to "gently lay thy head" but giving us a wake-up call. His words are a reminder that our fighting and controversy are a distraction. Our security has never been in the circumstances of this world or its people; it has always been in Jesus.

Notice how the second command after "Be still" is "know." In order for us to have a true understanding of who God is, we must silence ourselves before Him. This means letting go of all those chirping voices, jumping off the to-do-list train, and no longer retreating to God but rather retreating in God. When we stop and remember whom we serve, we will remember that security is always within our grasp.

Stillness also calls God's people to a new level of accountability with how they fight. When anger arises or retaliation feels necessary, being still provides the time to step back and remember the truth that God is moving. Yielding to God is our best war tactic even when it feels scary and uncertain to trust beyond what we see. "In awe"—that will always be our response when our eyes are opened to what He is doing in and around us. We stop trying to find the words or appropriate response. Our humbled heart is full of gratitude when we become still with Him.

Dear Lord, thank You for who You are. As we go about our day, can You help our heart remember the importance and necessity of being still? This is not a suggestion but rather a command You give us. Thank You for helping us silence our mind so that our eyes are fully opened to Your presence. We stand in awe of Your presence and holiness. In Jesus's name, amen.

Let Yourself Be Known

Bear one another's burdens,
and so fulfill the law of Christ.
GALATIANS 6:2 NKJV

There are certain emotions that are easier to express than others, aren't there? One that never gets easier no matter how old we become is loneliness.

It's confusing. We feel silly to feel lonely. In a world full of ways to connect, how is loneliness so prevalent? So easy? Depression, which is most commonly linked to loneliness, has skyrocketed in this age of heightened technology.

Have we mastered the ability to be popular and somehow not be known? Has the reality that we can virtually connect kept us from intimately knowing another?

We spend so much time crafting, protecting, creating, and perfecting our reputation or who others think we should be that we often don't let them get to know the real us. Right? And so while we may feel temporary satisfaction or excitement from relationships, we get to the end of the day and question their depth.

This has to break the heart of our Father. He sees us hurting, struggling, clawing, and yearning to be loved and known and yet watches us spend our energy trying to be someone we aren't. When we feel lonely or isolated, He reminds us that He is near. Never will He leave us; never will He forsake us. That, we can trust.

But He does not end there. He begs us to step into true connection with other believers. He hopes we stop doctoring our bruises and let another hear our story. He reminds us that perfecting our image impresses for a moment but letting Him perfect us in our weakness is the real treat. If we want to stop feeling isolated, we must let ourselves be known. We cannot live on an island and expect community. We must be vulnerable, trusting the Lord to cover our gaps and be our protection. True friendship requires breaking down our walls and stepping into the freedom of being completely and wholly ourselves.

Great hope is found when we accept the invitation to be intimately known by our Savior and to know His likeness in return.

Dear Jesus, thank You for giving us the courage to be open and the desire to be known. You formed our innermost being; we trust You to protect us, and we choose not to hide. Thank You for removing the "lonely" label and replacing it with "loved." In Jesus's name, amen.

Thoughts Overflow

Be careful how you think;
your life is shaped by your thoughts.
PROVERBS 4:23 GNT

The moment our feet hit the floor, our mind begins whirling with thoughts. Whether it be what we will say at our ten o'clock meeting, the creative ways we are going to make ourselves work out today, or how we are going to pay off all this debt, we begin thinking about one thing and then are bombarded with text messages, e-mails, or social media, prompting another slew of thoughts. As we do our best to sort through them and make coffee, the television airs breaking news of another event, and our brain feels like a jumbled-up mess.

There are so many things to think about, aren't there? It's like as soon as we set our mind on something, life offers another knock at the door with several more visitors that all want our attention.

Why are thoughts so important? Aren't actions all that matter? Jesus constantly talks about the importance of a healthy thought life, a life focusing on the eternal and not the here-and-now. He knows that what we fill our mind with will determine what we do, what we believe, and, ultimately, who we are. Our mind is capable of magnificent things. When we couple our talents with God's supernatural power, we set ourselves up to take part in miracles. But it all begins with what is in our head.

Do we fill our mind with unhealthy expectations for our relationships and then wonder why we always leave disappointed? Do we entertain gossip with others and then wonder why our friendships lack honesty and intimacy? Do we let money and pride drive our decisions and then wonder why we still feel empty?

If we want our life to change, we must start with our thought life. And if we want our thought life to change, we can only do it through His Word. As we make our focus the truth of His promises, we will be able to revitalize our thought life to reach our God-given potential.

Dear Jesus, thank You for giving us the power to choose our own thoughts. As we sift through what must stay and what must go, help us lean into Your truth and think thoughts that bring You glory. We want to have a healthy, innovative, and pure mind. In Jesus's name, amen.

Made New

Remember not the former things,
nor consider the things of old.
Behold, I am doing a new thing;
now it springs forth, do you not perceive it?
I will make a way in the wilderness
and rivers in the desert.
ISAIAH 43:18-19 ESV

Maybe today has been like off-the-charts great for you. Or maybe it feels like you should receive a trophy for "Worst Day Ever." Or maybe it just started and the canvas is blank, full of opportunity and possibility. Either way, there is really good news: tomorrow is a brand-spankin'-new day. Like fresh-sheets-out-of-the-dryer new—isn't that so incredibly nice to know?

No matter what happened yesterday, God promises that we don't have to dwell on the bruises, battle scars, or regrets of the past. So let's guard our thoughts, and when we wake up physically operating in the present but mentally consumed with the throes of yesterday (or even ten years ago), let's try to remember that God says our past experiences have been wiped clean.

Or what about our dreams? Our goals? The big, exciting things we had envisioned being our life—do they feel far from achievable? Unavailable to us because of mistakes we have made? We have accepted the lie that a once-tethered wing cannot fly again to new places, but why? We have taken our state of brokenness and stamped it as who we are: broken.

But what does Jesus say about us? And our life? Our goals? About our hurt wings and delicate past and all that lies in between?

We have been made new. That is what He says. Redeemed and restored—that is who we are.

This gift of newness repairs our broken wings, speaks life into our soul, and reminds our weary heart that our feet were never meant to stay on the ground.

Our today does not have to be the story of our tomorrow and our potential is not determined by our past. Gulp in that fresh air. It is good to be alive when Jesus is our King.

Dear Jesus, thank You that You are always making all things new. You speak to the potential within us, put the past behind us, and call us into Your marvelous light. We trust You to make a way. Reveal to us more of You, Jesus. We want to be made new. In Jesus's name, amen.

First a Follower

*It is the L*ORD *your God you must follow,*
and Him you must revere. Keep His commands
and obey Him; serve Him and hold fast to Him.
DEUTERONOMY 13:4 NIV

Remember the leadership award given at every middle school awards ceremony? Or the person on the football team elected to be team captain? Or the one voted to lead the strategy on the debate team? These positions of leadership were exciting to watch and especially exciting if we were the ones chosen. Being a leader—it feels important, significant, bold, self-assured, valued. Purposeful. It allows for a platform of influence and is a tangible sign of affirmation. It feels like recognition, and recognition feels good.

While being in a position of leadership is an honor and a high calling, we often forget that leaders are only made strong by the one they follow.

Leaders are followers, first and foremost. They have become leaders because they have learned to follow well. They are bold in their steps because they trust the One in front of them. They are assertive in their actions because they remain obedient to the One in control. They are confident in their own purpose because they do not look to the right or to the left, comparing themselves to another.

We can desire to be leaders for Jesus, and He wants that for us too, but if we desire to be a leader more than we crave being a follower of Him, both are compromised. We cannot prioritize anything above His glory; the moment we try to take the lead and forget that He is always ahead of us is the exact moment our own leadership on this earth is in jeopardy.

Jesus always relied on the strength of His Father. His lips continually voiced, "Your will, not mine." He remained obedient despite the rejection and doubts of others. He knew His reach was only as wide and as deep as His willingness to obey His Father. Walking with God is what makes us worthy to be followed. Let's not desire for others to see us, but rather let's live a life that boldly points others to Him. The most important thing about a leader is who they follow—always.

Dear Jesus, thank You for being the perfect example of a leader and a follower. Help us refuse the temptation to make our own name known and instead make great of who You are. Your impact is forever and Your love reaches all. Show us how to rest in You today. In Jesus's name, amen.

Be on the Scene

*Truly, truly, I say to you,
whoever believes in me
will also do the works that I do;
and greater works than these will he do,
because I am going to the Father.*

JOHN 14:12 ESV

Common sense tells us that if we are absent from a scene, we miss it, right? Whether that be our friend getting married, a family member having a baby, or a big celebration, if we are not there, we miss it. Logic, yes? But have we considered the fact that there might be celebrations, parties, and miracles we are not seeing in our own life because we are not being present in the moment?

Honestly, it seems easy not to show up these days. There is a large difference between showing up in a way that we are comfortable and showing up in the ways that challenge us and the way God is asking us to participate. How many times do you think we might have missed out on a miracle moment because we were late or lazy on the scene? Or we got stuck inside our own head? The anxiety we experienced or the fear we nursed became a red traffic light we never got past, and we coined it a loss.

We must open our eyes to what the Lord is asking and how He is directing us. We are given grace for every missed opportunity, but the consequence of missing it still remains. While He will make good of every situation, why would we choose to miss out on being part of that good right here, right now?

Sometimes, the miracle is Jesus allowing us to take part in moving mountains, serving others, and being part of a movement. Sometimes the miracle is Jesus healing us of our sickness or resolving an issue. But sometimes the miracle is Jesus transforming us from the inside, as we learn that His strength is made perfect in our weakness.

Regardless, we must be on the scene. We must be present. Nobody else can live out the plans He specifically crafted for us. But those big, awesome, miracle-filled plans require us to bring all that we are and to show up. He just needs us.

Dear Jesus, thank You for the plans You have crafted just for us. Will You help us to show up on the scene, ready and willing? Thank You for letting us take part in miracles. We're loving being on Your team. In Jesus's name, amen.

He Is God of All

One God and Father of all,
who is over all and through all and in all.
EPHESIANS 4:6 NIV

Our heart—how is it feeling today? A little worn? Or just busy thinking of all that is going on in life? As we approach our day, let us take a deep breath and remember that our hope is sealed and secured in His hands no matter what comes our way.

He is over everything. All of it. Our impending doctor's appointment. Our big exam. Our college decision. Our move to a new city. Our soccer game or track meet. Our financial situation, hardships, or obligations. Our marriage, whether blissful or dangerously on the rocks. Our miscarriage. Our family's intervention for the addiction. Our new business venture. Our search for purpose in our chosen career.

Anything. Everything. All. The big and the small. The exciting and the mundane. The things that please Him and the moments that break His heart. He is there. He made all, every single one. He sees us, especially the lost and the broken. He knows all, even what we try our best to hide or disguise. He carries all, through hardship and triumph and tragedy and victory. All. He provides the courage. The hope. The energy. The truth. The stamina. The tenacity. The drive. The grace. The love. All. All such things are given to us to sustain and provide, to move and to live, to follow every dream inside of us.

All. There is no decision, emotion, crossroads, or human heart where He is not present. Our submission to His authority is the issue, but His authority? It is great and mighty.

He is over our day. He is over our mistakes. He is over our worries. He is over what's next for us. The same One who created everything You see chooses to live inside us. Let us walk in the authority and the truth that He has done it all for us.

Dear Jesus, thank You for being so powerful, so mighty, and so true. There is nothing that we experience, fear, or do that could remove us from Your hands. When we find ourselves picking up the burdens or worrying about circumstances, remind us that we hope in You. You are above all, in all, and for all. We trust You in all. In Jesus's name, amen.

Better Because of the Fire

Their work will be shown for what it is, because the Day will bring it to light. It will be revealed with fire, and the fire will test the quality of each person's work.
I CORINTHIANS 3:13 NIV

When it comes down to it, do any of us ever *want* to feel uncomfortable? Stretched? Placed with our backs against the wall or put in an impossible situation? Common sense and human tendency prove that hardly any of us would choose these methods of refinement. Traveling through the fire is never a way we request to see His faithfulness. We plead for intervention on our behalf or the smallest glimpse that this battle we are fighting is temporary. We want to know that this will all be over, and soon.

The adult life of Job in the Bible feels like one constant fire. One after the other, he finds out that all his ten children, his livestock, and his servants have died. He then is cursed with a terrible skin disease. His wife tells him to defy God and give up, but Job refuses to let hopelessness be the theme of his life. While the fire Job endured was excruciating, humility and truth reminded him that the Lord is never without reason and that His purpose on earth will not be thwarted.

God was not worried about making Job's life easier so that he would believe a good God existed. Rather, He was most concerned with Job realizing that God is always the most powerful force in our life. When Job began to really grasp what the Lord was saying, he responded in awe. He stopped attempting to understand and started to worship. Job was never without hope. This, he knew, even when the world around him seemed to be falling apart. And now, he could put a finger on why that was—the God of hope had never, ever left him.

Traveling through the fire is nothing to be ashamed of or hidden for no one to know. That is courage and humanity. The fire gives us true empathy for others who are struggling and forces us to find refuge in God alone. We are stronger and more firmly planted in His promises because they kept us going. We never choose fire, but sometimes God allows it— not to become a better version of ourselves but to become a truer reflection of Him.

Dear God, thank You for being most concerned about the condition of our heart. Sometimes this means we endure the fire because refinement requires it. Help us to seek You, be quick to obey, and to firmly trust that You are at work. In Jesus's name, amen.

Refuse to Be Realistic; Do the Impossible

Ah, Lord God!
It is you who have made the heavens
and the earth by your great power
and by your outstretched arm!
Nothing is too hard for you.
JEREMIAH 32:17 ESV

How often do we put limits on God? It is not something we are adamantly saying, "Lord, You can't do this!"— but it is obvious in our actions and beliefs that we do not truly expect God to show up and blow us away. And because we are not intentionally seeking to push past what we know, we settle for what our little mind can conceive.

But then, Jesus. He comes in and immediately bursts our comfort bubble. He breathes new life into those fearful places and tells us to prepare for what's ahead. Why? Because it's big and it's mighty. Because it will often be dressed in overalls and hard work, require the entry fee of sacrifice and pride, and ask that we drop every single little thing that hinders us, including the expectations and thoughts of those around us.

Think about it—did people think Sarah and Abraham were total looney toons when they claimed God's promise of still having a child well into their senior years? Or what about Noah? Not a drop of precipitation had fallen on the earth, yet he began building the ark in anticipation of the flood. These people, these stories—what was it about them that landed them in the pages of the living Word?

They refused to be "realistic" because they believed in a God who was and is all about doing the impossible. He is a God of provision, sustenance, and multiplication. Where He asks and sends, He is there.

What would it look like to wholeheartedly trust God with every detail of your life? Let's not be realistic anymore. Let's remind our heart that if we received the call, then we are the only one who knows the directions and received the courage to pursue it. It would be a shame to miss out on doing the impossible because we were waiting for the agreement of others.

Dear Jesus, thank You for the ways You are calling us out of our comfort zones. Help us to focus on Your voice, forgetting what is expected or realistic. We want to fear You and nothing else. Thank You for choosing us to do the impossible. In Jesus's name, amen.

Remember Whose You Are

Behold, I have engraved you on the palms of my hands;
your walls are continually before me.

ISAIAH 49:16 ESV

As a child, getting lost in a grocery store is terrifying. The aisles seem to last forever and there are people all around. But when we are lost, we feel like we can only find those we are not looking for, right? And what does someone ask when they are trying to help us, telling by the terrified look in our eyes that we are obviously lost? They say, "Who are your parents?" They ask who we came with because that is the only way we will be found. In that moment, all that matters is whose we are, and if we can remember that and get back to whose we are, all will be okay.

The same goes for us in our daily life, except so many times when we are wandering down the aisle looking for pleasure of our own preference, we do not realize we are lost. We continue to walk away from whose we are, captivated by what is around us, temporarily enthralled by what we see. Until we realize we are far from home, unaware of how to get back there, and we panic. Instead of remembering what we learned as children, we try to find our way back based on our own name. We offer our accolades and our affirmations in exchange for what we hope is purpose. We know we are lost, but we have forgotten the clue to get home.

What is it again? Oh, yes, we must remember whose we are. When we are aimless or pursuing things that we know do not satisfy, the only remedy to finding ourselves again is to remember who created us. Who brought us here? Who is our Protector? Our heavenly Father. He is the voice that we long to hear and the face we have been praying to see. When we think we're longing for the comfort of home or familiarity or close friends or routine, what we're really longing for is the comfort of Jesus. When we walk through life knowing the Person that we've come with and the price that He paid for us, we walk with our head high and our heart confident. When we temporarily lose our way or get distracted, we look for Him. We say His name aloud and He shows Himself near. All we must do is remember whose we are; that is our way home.

Dear Jesus, thank You for calling us by name and never leaving our side. When our heart forgets who we are, will You set off the alarm in our soul to return to home base? Guide us down paths of righteousness. In Jesus's name, amen.

*"When the heart
and mind focus
on things unseen—
that's when there's a
visible change in us."*

ANN VOSKAMP

An Undivided Heart

Draw near to God and He will draw near to you.
Cleanse your hands, you sinners;
and purify your hearts, you double-minded.
JAMES 4:8 NKJV

When we tell someone, "You have my undivided attention," we are telling them that all our focus is on them, one hundred percent. We do not lay our phone on the table in anticipation of receiving a call or text. We do not browse the internet as they begin conversation. We awaken ourselves to the subject at hand, make ourselves aware of the context, and be present.

While our culture and its technological savviness can be beneficial in many ways, it has crippled many of us in our ability to be undivided. No matter where we are, we are not fully there. Even if physically committed, our mind is traveling. No matter how extraordinary the event we are attending, we experience the fear of missing out on everything else. How often do we do this with the Lord?

We imagine what we want for lunch while sitting

in church. We answer text messages in the middle of our quiet time. We attempt to focus our sights on Him yet find ourselves reacting to the urgencies of our day. We desire to put God first, but our priorities say otherwise. Our intention is to be undivided, but our attention, affection, and action split us in a million different ways.

If we really want to have a hopeful heart, we must put all our eggs in His basket. If our hope is divided, placing thirty percent in our resources or career and seventy percent in Jesus, then we are opening ourselves up to anxiety, fear, and disappointment.

Whatever area it is for us—career, family, appearance, money, dreams—let's recognize where we might have misplaced our hope and give it back to the only One capable of fulfilling us. And when we are tempted to be distracted or believe the lie that we can successfully divide our heart, let us remember what the Lord has asked of us all: everything.

Giving our attention fully to Him, we are able to walk in peace and hear His gentle nudges. Giving Jesus the affection He deserves, He in turn gives us the capacity to handle everything else with Him by our side.

Dear Jesus, thank You for being dependable, gracious, and selfless. When we are tempted to place our hope in places other than You, renew our mind. We trust Your faithfulness and know a divided hope is a wavering hope. In Jesus's name, amen.

What Does Hopeful Look Like?

But if we hope for what we do not yet have,
we wait for it patiently.
ROMANS 8:25 NIV

What does it mean to be hopeful? Is it constant optimism despite our circumstances? How do we cultivate it in our own life on a daily basis? Sometimes it looks like taking a leap of faith toward a dream that has been brewing in one's heart. Sometimes it looks like speaking words of promise out loud even when it feels like the circumstances are impossible. Sometimes it looks like continuing to plow the fields before us and being faithful in the monotonous.

However it specifically dresses itself, being hopeful does not remain stagnant in its current position. Even if the circumstance requires incredible patience, a heart that is hopeful is persistent in patience. We believe waiting on God to be a sedentary position, similar to us waiting on a bench until a bus arrives and we can safely travel to our desired destination. But being hopeful is not sitting on a bench; being hopeful is praying for every bus that comes to that stop and standing up, ready to jump on, if it is the correct one. It is proactively preparing oneself for the next adventure in the midst of the delay.

While hope is a choice we make on the inside, it is seen in our demeanor and our body language. It is made obvious by how we speak to others. It is apparent in our responses and our attitudes. When we believe that God is going to show up in the perfect timing, we cheerfully and obediently wait on Him. When fatigue or impatience want our attention, we spend time reminding our heart of His promises for our life.

"Lord, remind us You are working," we ask. Hopeful hearts experience discouragement, but they detect its poison. Bitterness does not stand a chance, and weariness is refreshed in the presence of the Lord.

Are we hopeful people when we are not getting what we want when we think we should get it? May we set our sights on Him, renew our strength with His power, and remind our soul that our bus is never early and never late but always right on time.

Dear Jesus, thank You for giving us a hopeful heart that brings glory to Your name. When we are frustrated or impatient, remind us to prepare and pray for what is ahead. Your timing is perfect and Your will is good. In Jesus's name, amen.

Not Just Valley Vernacular

"For I know the plans I have for you," declares the LORD,
"plans to prosper you and not to harm you,
plans to give you hope and a future."
JEREMIAH 29:11 NIV

Does it seem like the word *hope* is more rampant when tragedy strikes or unexpected circumstances knock on our door? The vernacular of *hope* is one we are used to depending upon when we are going through hard times. It seems more necessary then, right?

But God never intended for our hope to be reserved for the bad days or the trenches. He wants us to experience His hope in every moment, that it would be our music of praise at the mountaintop, our expression during the everyday, and our way during the wilderness.

A hopeful heart is a zestful heart. It seizes the ordinary with anticipation of the extraordinary. It is language coloring our canvas with promise and assurance, believing that our God is exactly who He says He is.

While it is important to have a reservoir of hope for the dry seasons, we must not bottle it up out of fear that it will run out. Hope manifests itself much like creativity does—the more it is used and explored, the more it appears. The gift is exercised and the supply grows. God's hope is not coming from a shallow pool but from the living Word of God, and it is a river that never runs dry.

In the good times, let us express to others the hope that forges our steps. And when life is steady, let us prepare for the hope that awaits us next and decide to still show up every day with excitement.

Do physically strong people build up their muscles in case their body has to fight off a disease? Or is it so their everyday life can be made stronger, more proactive, and fuller in measure? Their desire to be their best self is not in the case of tragedy but rather because of the hope that lies in the present. Let us treat our hope the same way. Let our words be ones of life and our prayers remain constant.

Dear God, thank You for giving us this wonderful life! We want to be people of hope who speak kind words, believe in big dreams, and courageously go forth in Your name. Help us to not hoard our hope but rather use it now, trusting You to replenish all. In Jesus's name, amen.

So Many Unanswered Prayers

For the LORD God is our sun and our shield.
He gives us grace and glory.
The LORD will withhold no good thing
from those who do what is right.

PSALM 84:11 NLT

For the longest time, my mom has been begging me to keep a journal. Every time we get together and begin talking about what we have learned and how God has been speaking to us, she will say, "Cleere, I have been telling you since you were sixteen to keep a journal; when are you going to listen? You won't remember all these moments, and you will want to."

How often are our mothers correct? Too often, it seems. I finally started keeping one. I suppose a "log" is a more correct term, as some days it has mere bullet points of emotions I am feeling or concerns I am having. Less than six months have passed and I can already see a pattern—God really does have our best interests at heart.

This is hard to believe sometimes though, isn't it? Based on what our human eyes can see, the circumstances surrounding us feel impossible. We read His promises and feel like He has forgotten us.

"Lord, do You see? Please answer my prayer. I can't do this," we clamor. And sometimes He remains silent on the surface.

But what my log has reminded me is that behind the scenes, oh, He is working miracles. While answered prayers reinvigorate the human spirit and push us onward, I believe it is in the unanswered prayers that we can truly see His provision and sovereignty.

We think we know what we need, but we tend to confuse that with what we desire.

We think we know the best route, but we tend to forget our limited vision.

We think we are incapable, but we forget that His strength is made perfect in our weakness.

His faithfulness is not up for question and His goodness is unmatched. He does not withhold good from His children; rather, He gives abundant life as He helps us redefine what "good" truly means.

Dear God, thank You for being King of our heart and our life. You are faithful and kind, and we trust in Your promises. When our mind wants to doubt, lead us back to Your Word and remind us of Your character. As we lift our requests and prayers to you, we trust that You will respond in Your perfect power. In Jesus's name, amen.

No Time for Offense

Good sense makes one slow to anger,
and it is his glory to overlook an offense.
PROVERBS 19:11 ESV

How often do we get offended? Think about this for a moment. How often do we see remarks of offense written on Facebook's newsfeed, repeated on the daily news, sent through text messages, or heard within the hallways of our workplace? We are an offended generation, which has made us a very defensive generation.

This constant state of offense keeps us from being effective. Instead of seeing the world as a whole and looking from an eternal perspective, it makes us zoom in and evaluate situations and relationships based on our feelings alone. However it affected our pride, this bruising takes our focus from serving and loving others to self-preservation. What we view as defending ourselves eventually becomes a barrier, where we cannot accurately see the world around us. We are not wrong for experiencing (sometimes intense) emotions during these moments. However, if we continually react based solely on our feelings and only consider our own viewpoint, we will have few friends and a volatile family dynamic, and our world will be reduced to the size of our own bubble.

Before we take offense to the words and actions of others, we must take the time to be still and not react. Consider when we might have spoken out of line, talked negatively, excluded another, or any other offensive thing—haven't there been moments? Was it a true and accurate reflection of our feelings about that person? Did we let the issues of our heart boil over and affect those around us?

More than likely, yes. Wouldn't it behoove us to remember this wisdom when we ourselves are offended? We have much to do in this world—places to go, dreams to achieve, people to help, and a God to serve. If our hands are balled up in fists protecting ourselves or we're too busy gathering bricks to build a wall, we will waste so much time.

We are responsible for what we receive, what we replace, what we reject, and how we respond. Let us stop wearing our heart on our sleeve so that we can utilize every moment to share the heart of our heavenly Father.

Dear Jesus, thank You for the gift of a sound mind. Will You remind us that offense is a choice, and that even when our pride is bruised, we can count on You to rebuild us? We will not let our emotions be our guide. In Jesus's name, amen.

Hopeful on a Tightrope

Why are you cast down, O my soul, and why are you in turmoil within me? Hope in God; for I shall again praise him, my salvation and my God.
PSALM 43:5 ESV

Is it possible to be hopeful in the midst of total chaos?

Is it realistic to believe that our future is bright when life feels like doom and gloom?

Is it wise to continue a course when the world is telling us there is no way we can get across?

Although we would all prefer for life to remain as sunshine and rainbows, no one is silly enough to believe that it will be our reality. Our dearest family members go to be with Jesus far before we are emotionally ready to let them go. Marriages are devastated by the discovery of affairs, tearing apart the fabric of what everyone believed was the perfect family. Health conditions are revealed that force some to change their dreams and reconstruct their life. Financial hardships storm past our doors without knocking, offering no mercy or patience as we try to remedy how we are going to move forward.

Life is hard. Full of transition and adjustment, the waves continuously come upon the shore just as we stumble to our feet again. Is it naive to believe in the goodness of God when the difficulties of life scream anything but?

While hope seems easier to have when circumstances are good, the truest test of a hopeful heart is on the tightrope. It is here that we depend on and witness the depth of His goodness and grace. While never preferred, the tightrope is the most intimate and immediate way to experience the presence of God. As He watches our legs shake, He extends His hand and opens our eyes to the horizons ahead. As we place one foot in front of the other, we are forced to remain in the present and place our hope in the One holding our hand.

The beauty of life on a tightrope, when each step feels daunting and unsure, is that we must rely on Jesus. There is simply no alternative. While on the surface a solution feels elusive, the desperation and yearning that we experience in these places is actually right where Jesus wants us to be.

Dear Jesus, thank You for the hardship, heartbreak, and hopelessness we feel in this life; they remind us that You really are our only Hope. Hold us close today. Warm our hearts as we remember that You never let us go. In Jesus's name, amen.

Comparing Potholes

*Examine yourselves, to see whether you are
in the faith. Test yourselves.
Or do you not realize this about yourselves,
that Jesus Christ is in you?—
unless indeed you fail to meet the test!*
II CORINTHIANS 13:5 ESV

In a world that has confused value with worldly affirmation, purpose with visible success, and fulfillment with the acquisition of material things, it makes sense that it is hard for us to not get caught up in the vortex of wanting and having "more."

Whether it be the clothes we are wearing, the number of children we have, our career path, or the number of times we have done our Bible study homework, we find a way to gauge our own progress and value based on those around us. We immediately turn our head to examine the lives of those around us when we experience a disappointment. "Why me, Lord?" we question.

We assume we understand the struggles surrounding us, and we respond with envy, wondering why our path has to be so much harder than those who walk alongside us. We compare potholes, secretly wishing for those around us to endure what we did or praying that our road becomes smooth like theirs. This is not what God wants for us!

God's strength within us provides the ability to handle whatever our journey entails no matter how difficult that may be. Every person is different, which means that we must be refined and transformed in different ways. The plans He will unfold for each of His children will never look the same.

When we let our focus be compromised by the blessings or burdens of those around us, we are placing our hope in our circumstances and doubting the wisdom of our heavenly Father. Have we forgotten that we are royalty? Chosen. Equipped. We are destined to do great works in His name and love as He does. Let us keep our eyes on the road ahead, using all our energy to run our race well for the glory of our King.

Dear Jesus, thank You that You are a good, good Father. You give and You take away, and we trust all Your hands do. Help us place our security in You. Remind our heart that the potholes keep us alert and redirect our hope to You. We choose to keep our gaze fixed ahead and not become distracted by the path of those around us. In Jesus's name, amen.

Freedom at His Feet

Humble yourselves, therefore,
under the mighty hand of God
so that at the proper time he may exalt you,
casting all your anxieties on him,
because he cares for you.
I PETER 5:6–7 ESV

We go and we go and we go.

We do and we do and we do.

We give and we give and we give.

We run and we strive and we hustle, and we are all tired. Anxious. Unfulfilled. Our feet are moving, but the gear to our heart health is so jammed in overdrive, we have forgotten what is normal.

This is not a "shaming the millennials/technology-saturated generation" devotion—but a frequently seen trend is worth paying attention to, right?

Why are we this way? And how do we stop? Will we ever feel settled?

Anxiety will always find a way in when our strength, trust, or hope are placed in anything besides God. First Peter 5:6–7 tells us to "humble yourselves" in these moments of anxiety, meaning that our anxiety usually stems from placing ourselves on a pedestal we do not deserve and obviously cannot handle.

Think about it—when are we anxious? When we try to take matters into our hands, right? We do our best to manipulate circumstances to fit our own preferences. We plan for the future based on our limited perspective. We give all that we have to predicting the next moment, only to realize that we are not in control. The grip we thought we had on our family, finances, future, etc., has shriveled to nothing.

It is in these moments that we must take our rightful place at the throne of Jesus. What is over our head is at His feet. And despite the millions of times He has asked us to lay it down, He will gladly take it the moment we decide to listen. Freedom is ours at His feet. Letting anxiety go is acknowledging the authority that is rightfully His.

Our pride has kept our blistered hands holding on for too long. But there is relief for us here...a way to travel that is light and sure. All we must do is show up at His feet, be still in His presence, and be reminded that our cares are in the care of the King.

Thank You, Jesus, for Your willingness to take our burdens and lift our fears. When we feel our heart getting anxious, quickly remind us that You are in control. Help us stay at Your feet; we trust You with everything. In Jesus's name, amen.

Capturing Key Moments

And I heard the voice of the Lord, saying,
"Whom shall I send, and who will go for us?"
Then I said, "Here am I. Send me!"
ISAIAH 6:8 ESV

Key moments. Critical moments. Moments that changed the game for us. We can all think of a few right off the bat; whether we have missed the opportunity or shown up swinging, these key moments have been crucial in the trajectory of our life.

That employee we saw being excluded and took the initiative to invite them to lunch? As we look over our wedding pictures and see their face, we realize the key moment that we made a lifelong friend.

That conversation we had with our siblings that placed us in the perfect position to be vulnerable and transparent about our struggles? As we accept our diploma, we look up and see them in the stands—and remember the moment we invited them in, accepting their support and opening up a new level of accountability for ourselves.

That job opportunity we felt incapable of

attaining but filled out the application anyway? As we were promoted for the second time and became a manager of others, we are humbled by the grace and knowledge God ushered along the way.

Isn't it crazy how a moment in time can change the way life turns out? God is all about creating these moments for us, but it is up to us to follow through with them.

He gave us the Holy Spirit, living and active inside each of us, so that we may hear Him and discern what His will is from moment to moment. He gave us His Word so that we may know what He desires for us and the people He has called us to be. When we allow ourselves to be still and seek Him, we place ourselves in position to hear His voice and respond with courage. He has called each of us, with our unique makeup, experience, and background, to represent Him. And nothing can stop us from accomplishing what He has planned for us. Let us take hold of every key moment, fully trusting God with the final outcome.

Dear Jesus, thank You for every opportunity You place before us. Will You help us to be aware and willing, not letting a single key moment pass us by? We are grateful for Your boldness in using us. In Jesus's name, amen.

The Sabbath: Not a Suggestion

*By the seventh day God had finished
the work He had been doing;
so on the seventh day He rested from all His work.*
GENESIS 2:2 NIV

The sun, the stars, and the moon.

The animals that swim the seas, inhabit the rain forest, and roam the earth.

The grass that grows beneath our feet so that we may walk with instant cushion.

The color of our eyes, the angle of our nose, the way we move and have our being. Every human who has ever walked the face of the planet or will ever do so—God. He made it all.

Everything beautiful is His creation.

And yet He rested. Read the entire verse: "By the seventh day God had finished," as in past tense. His diligence was perfect and His power incomprehensible. He did the work that was necessary. But once it was complete, He took the time to be still. He knew what was needed, and once it was finished, He disciplined Himself in holiness.

If our perfect God needed the Sabbath, wouldn't it make sense that we do too?

Our to-do lists will always offer up opportunities to be distracted. Our perfectionistic nature will beckon us to keep our hands moving, our productivity flowing, and our schedules finely etched.

But this day of rest is a gift! More often than not, our productivity is compromised by our lack of awareness and focus, which is only heightened through rest. We were created to have this time to recharge, to restore our body, renew our mind, and refill our cup. There is no pressure to receive anything; it is simply to be.

Delighting in the discipline of the Sabbath will not only keep our priorities in line and put a smile on our heavenly Father's face, but it will also provide the stamina and strength we need to do the rest of our week well. It is these moments of doing nothing that we discover we are much more than what we do. When we give our first to Jesus and give this time to Him and to ourselves, He replenishes our time and provides all that we need to walk out His will.

Dear Jesus, thank You for the gift of the Sabbath. Will You help us to see this day for what it is—a time of rest and renewal in You? We delight in this time with You as we let Your love wash over us. In Jesus's name, amen.

"Remember whose you are and whom you serve. Provoke yourself by recollection and your affection for God will increase tenfold; your imagination will not be starved any longer but will be quick and enthusiastic, and your hope will be inexpressibly bright."

OSWALD CHAMBERS

The Power of the Subconscious

The end of all things is at hand;
therefore be self-controlled and sober-minded
for the sake of your prayers.
I PETER 4:7 ESV

Imagine an ocean—what do we see? The waves crashing along the shoreline...the vastness of the waters extending beyond what we can see...the waves rippling across the shore.... We witness the lives the ocean holds when they lift their heads above the water and feel the breeze before returning to the majesty beneath. It's breathtaking, isn't it?

While the view is captivating, we are aware that the only reason we see beauty at the surface of the water is because of what is housed below it. In fact, what we see is the smallest, tiniest morsel of the beauty; the true magic is deep below the waters.

This is very similar to the human mind, soul, and heart. While our emotions are what we express to others, the complex intricacies of who we are extend far beyond what we feel. And so when we talk about hope—finding it, sowing it, cultivating it, harvesting it, and living it—it will be a result of the beauty beneath the surface.

The subconscious mind is like a storehouse, receiving and storing data so that our conscious mind forms the correct thoughts, responses, and actions in our everyday life. As we seek to be people who follow Jesus with no qualms or questions, we must realize the power that our mind plays in storing this hope.

What are we listening to? What music or audio do we turn on—in the car, while working, or when working out? Who are we hanging out with? Our associations matter deeply. Regardless of whether we think we will fall into the habits of those who surround us, good or bad, they affect our own habits.

What are we reading or watching on television? Who do we follow on social media? All these things matter. Much like the ocean, the life and beauty that others see in us is a mere reflection of the deeper chambers of our existence.

Dear Jesus, thank You for the power of our mind and that we get to choose what surrounds us on a daily basis. Help us keep watch over our ears, eyes, hands, and feet. Let us seek wisdom and truth in every area of our life. In Jesus's name, amen.

The Force of Hope in Warfare

"No weapon that is formed against you will prosper;
and every tongue that accuses you in judgment you will
condemn. This is the heritage of the servants of the LORD,
and their vindication is from Me," declares the LORD.
ISAIAH 54:17 NASB

Spiritual warfare is one of those topics that is hard to fully comprehend. We like to be able to envision things, to understand situations, to imagine the reality—but spiritual warfare? We will never understand it in its entirety.

Some people fear talking about it, believing their acknowledgment of the battle will make it worse. Maybe if we do not pay attention to it, it will just disappear. But pretending there is not a fight for our heart, our mind, and our soul doesn't make it go away. If we do not realize the dire need to guard our mind and take up our sword, we are leaving an open invitation for the enemy to come right through the front door.

How do we prevent this from happening? We don't want to be paranoid, fearful followers who never enjoy our blessings. We must open our eyes to the hope that is found in Jesus, the Author and Perfector of our faith. Hope is much like the insurance coverage on our armor. Ephesians tells us to put on the armor of God—the belt of truth, the breastplate of righteousness, the sandals of peace, the shield of faith, the helmet of salvation, the sword of the Spirit, and the prayer that holds them all together.

When we clothe ourselves in this armor, we are saying to the King of heaven's armies that we trust in the Eternal Hope. When the enemies seem stacked against us and the battle feels impossible, the force of hope is our strongest weapon.

An insurance policy is necessary on anything that is valuable. That is what hope does for the human spirit. It ensures that no matter the battle our armor endures, the cost of our life has been paid in full, and it is protected by the name of Jesus Christ.

Hope is our greatest form of strategic offense in spiritual warfare. If the goal of the war is victory and ours has already been established, then reminding our heart of this promise allows us to fight passionately and confidently.

Dear Jesus, thank You for the opportunity to fight the good fight. As we go about our days, can You remind us that war is waging around us but our hope makes us secure? Show us how to be victorious in every moment. In Jesus's name, amen.

Hope for the Future, Used in the Now

Let us hold unswervingly to the hope we profess,
for He who promised is faithful.
HEBREWS 10:23 NIV

During one of my first jobs, I began putting some money aside into a retirement account. It was not a normal savings fund that could be accessed at any time; this fund required that I reach a certain age before I could access it.

While I knew that investing in a retirement fund was a wise decision, it was hard to discipline myself to put aside money that would be helpful to me now so that I would have a more comfortable life down the road. It was for the future, with no accessibility or aid in the present. This is a good picture of how our faith operates. While we may not be able to see all the benefits of following Jesus while we're on earth, our love for Jesus will eventually result in us getting to spend eternity with Him. Our hope in Jesus is timeless. It is the vessel that carries us through all our days, keeping our focus on Him.

When we choose to see hope as elusive or something that is not "useful" to us, we are forgetting what it really means to have hope in God.

Hope in God allows us to embrace the heartache we experience with loss and rejection, knowing that we trust in a God who makes all things come together for our good.

Hope in God provides us with the courage to seize the opportunities we are given on this earth to make a true difference. It reminds us that our reputation and riches are short-lived but His kingdom is forever.

Hope in God soothes every anxiety we will ever have, trusting that He knows who we need and what we need when we need it. We are aware that He is for us, fighting on our behalf. He is our Comforter.

Hope in God is how we fight now; it is the anchor we hold tightly to, knowing that He will not leave our side.

Hope in God turns every challenge and hardship into an opportunity to see our King work miracles. Because we have an assurance of victory and a place reserved for us for eternity, the unexpected valleys and seasons of uncertainty cannot claim our destiny.

Hope in God is everything. The only way we can make an impact in our world today is to place our hope in the kingdom that is to come.

Dear Jesus, thank You for the gift of hope. We know it is our everyday resource that allows us to fight the good fight of faith. Thank You for being our anchored foundation; You are faithful. In Jesus's name, amen.

The Hustle Is Sexy

What you have learned and received and heard
and seen in me—practice these things,
and the God of peace will be with you.
PHILIPPIANS 4:9 ESV

How often do we find ourselves lusting after a different or simpler life? The attainment of riches is so close we can taste it, and we want more. The acquiring of prestigious relationships and that clout we have been searching for—we must admit, it feels good. The parties are fun. The house is beautiful. The car drives like a champ. The college degree feels important. The prestige is alluring.

We chase after fulfillment and let this false hope become our God. Unfortunately, it's not until we reach the "pinnacle," or goal, that we realize it's still not enough. And so there is this gap between our current reality and the one we wish was ours. This gap becomes our identity. Consciously and subconsciously, we center our life around reaching the destination.

But many of those who reach the highest levels in riches, careers, and popularity discover that no matter how much they accomplish, they feel lonely, empty, and unfulfilled. Why? Maybe because the harvest they planted was for the sake of themselves.

Solomon, the richest man to ever walk on this side of heaven, was worth billions and billions of dollars. And at the end of his life, Solomon says, "'Meaningless! Meaningless!' says the Teacher. 'Everything is meaningless!'" (Ecclesiastes 12:8 NIV). Solomon had hustled, recruited others to hustle for him, and been given every resource, relationship, and thing he could ever ask for—and yet he deemed it meaningless. Isn't it a shame that we spend so much time being fooled by the glitter and miss the true gold found in the goodness of our God?

The hustle is sexy because it advertises a life that is not real. And whether we like to face it or not, the enemy hopes we will run hard after it, compromising our destiny and our truth. But we have seen those before us, heard the words of Solomon, and experienced the deep, empty feeling in our own stomach. Let us be people who abandon the call to make ourselves known and seek to make Jesus famous. In that, we will find life.

Dear Jesus, thank You that you offer grace for every moment we run after things that are not of You. Help us glean the wisdom we have learned, removing the pressures of this world and trusting in the abundant life You have for us. In Jesus's name, amen.

Recognize Your Village

Therefore comfort each other and edify one another,
just as you also are doing.
I THESSALONIANS 5:11 NKJV

Do you ever find yourself focusing on the relationships you wish you had—or wondering if you need more? It's funny how twisted our perspective can become when our focus is off. We can barely maintain the relationships we have without feeling as if something is out of balance, and yet we feel the need to cultivate more.

This pressure has leaked into the way we serve and love others. Instead of seeing and expressing appreciation for who they are in our life, we use that energy to worry about whoever isn't there.

Our heart desires intimacy and quality, but we let the worry of our reputation keep us striving. We want all the likes and all the claps and all the friends and all the support, and we basically want our village to not really be a village—we want everyone in it.

But here's the deal: Jesus had twelve disciples. The only perfect Being did not surround Himself with everybody He could find, nor did He concern Himself with those who rejected Him. He served and loved everyone, yes. But when He was with them? It was enough. His mind didn't wander. They knew He was grateful for them.

How are we doing with this? Are we appreciating those who show up for us? Has intimacy, discernment, and gratitude directed our way in our relationships? God is the greatest dot connector ever. He can place someone in our path in a moment and change their heart in a second. He knows who we need and when we need them. Our role is to appreciate the people He places in our path.

We need to thank our village. Hug them. Speak life into them. Recognize their investment. When we make it our priority to be still so that we can gain awareness of the needs that surround us, we sow hope into the lives of others.

Dear Jesus, thank You for every person You've divinely placed into our life. Help us recognize and appreciate them for all they are to us. Thank You for displaying Your goodness and grace in the relationships You place in our paths. We trust You to connect every dot. In Jesus's name, amen.

The Allure of Gentleness

Let your gentleness be evident to all.
The Lord is near.
PHILIPPIANS 4:5 NIV

When we describe God or imagine Him in our mind, what words usually come to mind? We think of how mighty and powerful He is. We think of His selflessness, faithfulness, and grace. However, we often forget to include His gentleness. It seems like a less-important quality, one that gets mixed in alongside *gracious* or *true*.

Gentleness is far different. When someone is completely gentle in nature without compromising one bit of truth, it is the rarest combination of all. Gentleness is more than a soft touch; it is the warmth and welcoming of a soft touch while also being a firm hand. That is what God is for us. His gentleness is what provided the way for Him to eat with tax collectors, speak to the lost and the broken, and gain the respect of any earthly king. Because when someone is truly sovereign, there is no convincing or persuasion necessary to exert their authority.

God has never been in jeopardy of not being God; He has never had to compromise His gentleness to exert His force. His love is not conditional or abrasive but rather inviting and gentle. He asks us to be the same way—humble in approach and gentle in delivery.

The hope of God is always delivered in gentleness. It is clothed in such a way that it warms even the hardest of hearts. That is why it looks so different than the world's truth. It considers the receiver, makes known to itself the circumstances around it, and arrives in a way that no one questions the authenticity of the source. Gentleness is not the absence of reason or logic; it is the very presentation of it in a way that others can actually hear.

Let us be gentle in spirit and humble in nature. Quieting our own voices and submitting to the thoughtfulness of God will allow us to share the gospel in a profound way that will delight even the coldest of hearts. The allure of gentleness—it is the very reason He drew us in.

Dear Jesus, thank You for Your gentle nature and confident spirit. As we travel through our day, let our gentleness be evident to all. Remove any harshness within us and give us Your demeanor and delivery. In Jesus's name, amen.

Drenched in Love

See what great love the Father has lavished on us,
that we should be called children of God!
And that is what we are! The reason the world
does not know us is that it did not know Him.

I JOHN 3:1 NIV

We receive our evaluation back and instantly smile, thinking to ourselves, "Oh, yes! He will be pleased."

We look in the mirror and see that our skin is finally looking as dewy as the magazines. Our body has also slimmed down. "Getting there," we think.

We are recognized in church for our service and compassion. "Did You hear that?" we ponder as we look up at Him.

Do any of these sound familiar, our yearning attempts to earn the love of our heavenly Father? We often do not even realize what we are doing, as we have spent so long striving to earn a love that surpasses all understanding. Usually we cannot comprehend why He would give it to us—and so freely. Especially after we mess up...over and over again.

The Father's love for us is so mighty. It breaks down any barrier we have formed against it. It is all-knowing; it understands our thoughts before we form them; and it loves us despite ourselves. It eliminates our shame. It sends our fear packing. It reinvigorates our confidence and restores our faith. It is the basis of every bit of hope we have within our heart, because it is the only thing in this life that will never run dry. It is for every person in every place, because He made every heart. It is wide-reaching and full and certain.

Although we are extraordinary in His sight, we do not have to do anything extraordinary to earn His love. It is what we receive simply by being His. May we not worry ourselves trying to bottle it up, fearing it will run out. And may we not let our mind put a lid on what is uncontainable. It is a mighty rushing river that drenches every human heart. What a loving God we serve.

Dear Jesus, thank You for Your crazy love for Your children. We will always come up short when trying to deserve Your love; help us accept it and embrace every drop. You are our Redeemer, our Rock, and our greatest love. We choose to sit and soak in Your love today. In Jesus's name, amen.

Hope Found in Forgiveness

Bear with each other and forgive one another
if any of you has a grievance against someone.
Forgive as the Lord forgave you.
COLOSSIANS 3:13 NIV

Think back on a time when forgiveness was offered to you and you knew you were completely unworthy of it? It screamed of grace and selflessness and represented Jesus so well.

The fact that we can call up these memories so quickly is because they deeply affected us; we were not just witnesses to the miracle of true forgiveness, we were beneficiaries of it.

And what is even more beautiful than receiving that kind of forgiveness is being the one to offer it to someone else.

Forgiveness is fun to talk about and feels holy to explore. At the foundation of the Christian faith, it is a core principle of holiness. But offering it to someone when they have broken your heart, rejected you, betrayed you, gossiped about you, or worse—forgiveness then becomes a task far too lofty for your comfort zone. We claim grace, but our mind fights for retaliation. We want to make sense of it.

And then we remember how much He forgives us. The brutal reality of our humanity and its entitled ways hit us square in the face, and we are so thankful that Jesus chooses to look past what we do because He knows who we are. Through this washing-away, our home becomes evident.

He continues to use us, love us, claim us, and fight for us. His forgiveness is strong and all-encompassing. Nothing overpowers it. Forgiveness is a blanket that removes our fears from yesterday and secures us in the present. It wraps around the depth of our heart and tangibly shows us what love is.

When we drive past our own pride and reluctance to give what is not deserved or even requested, we open the door that ushers in the deepest hope we will ever know. Offering forgiveness to others is a direct reflection of Jesus, and it shows His love in a very personal way—not just to us but to the person receiving forgiveness and those watching on the sidelines.

Dear Lord, thank You for washing us as white as snow and making us blameless in Your sight. Give us the strength and grace to forgive others as You have forgiven us. We want to be radical in our forgiveness, lavishly offering it to those in need. We do not deserve Your grace, but we humbly walk in it. In Jesus's name, amen.

But It Seems So Simple

But I am afraid that, as the serpent deceived Eve by his craftiness, your minds will be led astray from the simplicity and purity of devotion to Christ.
II CORINTHIANS 11:3 NASB

When an answer seems too simple, it can feel like we are missing something. There has to be a flip side to this, right? If this is the answer, why isn't everyone doing it? If this is the correct path, why is everyone not following along?

When we get down to it, the crux of the gospel is simple. God is love, and He is truth. He sent His Son to die on the cross so that we may be forgiven of our sins. And in this exchange of the greatest grace we have ever known, we received the gift of eternal life. Now, let's tell others and let our life be a testament to this love in how we love, how we serve, how we give, and who we are.

His Word is full of instructions to guide us along the way, but the gist is simple: He just asks for our surrender and trust.

But the enemy will do his best to try to convince

us that the gospel is far too complex. Satan will take the immeasurable love of Christ and do his best to assure us that it is measurable and must be earned. He will take hold of our weaknesses, feast on our failures, and water our doubts, hoping we will find the gospel too intricate and too complex to believe.

But we know better. Sometimes it requires us getting to the point where we have exhausted all other answers and strategies and we are left asking, "Can He really love me in this place? Can He really fix this?"

Yes. Stillness in Jesus really is the answer to our futile running. And the moment when our thirst is quenched by His love and our soul steps into the healing of His presence, we will ask, "If all I had to do was stop, why did it take me so long?"

Let's not make this too complicated. His love is our remedy. His truth is our guide. His hope is our fortress. His presence is our peace.

Dear Jesus, thank You for being exactly who You say You are. You are not confusing or uncertain; You are steady and true. Help our heart be anchored in Your Word. Let us remove the webs and the extra words. Let the simplicity of You bring us back home. In Jesus's name, amen.

Sun Stands Still?

So the sun stood still and the moon stayed in place until the nation of Israel had defeated its enemies.

JOSHUA 10:13 NLT

How often does our fear hold us back from pursuing what we know God to be asking of us?

The Bible is full of stories that display the power of God when we jump headfirst into whatever is causing us to be afraid—and these stories are profound. Hard to imagine, even.

One story in particular is when Joshua and the Israelites defeated the southern armies (Joshua 10). Joshua and his men had been fighting kings and kingdoms and winning by a landslide. To save themselves, the people of Gibeon decided not to fight the successful warriors, but to become allies with them. So the Gibeonites made a treaty with Joshua and the Israelites. (Joshua 9). Shortly after they signed the treaty, Joshua was advised that five Amorite kings had joined forces to attack his new allies.

The Lord told Joshua not to be afraid of the five

Amorite kings, "Do not be afraid of them...for I have given you victory over them" (Joshua 10:8 NLT). Joshua proceeded to travel to Gibeon throughout the night and attacked the Amorite armies by surprise. To keep pursuing victory, Joshua asked the Lord to make the sun stand still so that there would be light.

The Lord answered Joshua's prayer, and the Israelites defeated their enemies. Imagine being Joshua. With every swing of your sword and every look into the sky, you are reminded that the Lord of heaven's armies is fighting for you and holding His creation still just for you.

What would happen if we lived as if we were not afraid? What would happen if we approached our days with unusual boldness and fought expecting our God to show up and show off?

If we really believe in the God of the Bible and claim to follow Him, daring is our only mode of operation. Audacious. Bravely obedient. Because we know that when we pray to the God of the universe for things that seem impossible and unrealistic, it is the perfect opportunity to see Him make miracles happen.

Dear Jesus, thank You for how You go before us and fight on our behalf. Help us to be like Joshua, having the courage to lead the way and trusting You to make the sun stand still on our path. In Jesus's name, amen.

*"Are you tired? Worn out?
Burned out on religion?
Come to me. Get away with me
and you'll recover your life.
I'll show you how to take a real
rest. Walk with me and work
with me—watch how I do it.
Learn the unforced rhythms
of grace. I won't lay anything
heavy or ill-fitting on you. Keep
company with me and you'll learn
to live freely and lightly."*

MATTHEW 11:28–30, THE MESSAGE

Work Your Land

Those who work their land will have abundant food,
but those who chase fantasies have no sense.
PROVERBS 12:11 NIV

Throughout Scripture, the metaphor of a farmer is used frequently—the planting of the crops, the tilling of the land, the waiting time as they grow, the harvest that is produced, the diligence of the farmer, and the faithfulness of God amid the entire process.

Because we are such an instant-gratification culture and society, the concept and timeline of farming gets lost on us. We now have express pickups at the grocery store, paper towels delivered to our doorstep, and almost any movie at the click of a button. While technology has made us efficient in some areas, it has trained our mind to think that the rest of the world works the same way.

But this is simply not the case. Just as our moms have told us, unfortunately, anything worth having takes hard work. We know this. When we sweat and give our all to whatever our hands are working on or whatever our mind is creating, we value the sacrifice of hard work. We appreciate the results, respect the process, and take greater delight in the harvest.

We know these are truths, and yet we often find ourselves still praying for overnight success. We want the beach body after working out for a week. We want the dream job as soon as we graduate from college. We want our family to be restored as soon as we sign up for counseling. Our desires begin to consume us, and despite our best attempt at keeping wisdom close, we begin to run wild, chasing fantasies of what could or should be

While dreaming *big*, impossible, God-sized dreams is never, ever a bad thing, it would be silly to think that these dreams come to fruition without determination. Worthwhile results require a true investment.

The Lord tells us in Proverbs that those who "work their land" will have abundant food. Whatever our lot is, whatever we have been given, we must manage it well. When we remain diligent in our days and keep our expectations placed on His Word, the harvest will be plentiful. A hopeful heart works the land, trusting in the Creator to provide.

Dear Jesus, thank You for reminding us of the importance of hard work. When we find ourselves craving instant gratification or forming false expectations, redirect us to Your hopes for us—that we may be diligent and steadfast in all we do. In Jesus's name, amen.

Flipping the Script

*The tongue has the power of life and death,
and those who love it will eat its fruit.*
PROVERBS 18:21 NIV

Perspective One: I am dreading work today.
Perspective Two: I have a job!

Perspective One: Everyone depends on me to do everything, and I'm exhausted.
Perspective Two: I may be worn out, but it is because I have so many people in my life whom I love and have the opportunity to serve.

Perspective One: I thought I would be married with kids by now.
Perspective Two: My situation allows me to volunteer, to give my best to my job, and to be there for my family. I know that God is aware of my desires.

Isn't the difference remarkable? It is not a question of "How do I change my circumstances?" but rather, "How do I see my circumstances in a different light?"

Perspective is the pathway to being a person of

praise or a person of pity. We get to decide whether we are going to play victim in the circumstances of our life or claim victory over what we believe regardless of what we see.

When our lips are busy praising God, even in the smallest of details, we no longer have time to rehearse pity. And what we practice, we perfect.

If we want to remain disappointed, frustrated, and bitter, we can keep Perspective One going. Or we can flip the script, choose to see the good in every situation, and speak life into our circumstances.

Believe it or not, our body hears the words we say, and it listens. If our lips speak doom and gloom, our posture will become sluggish and unsure and a frown will form far too easily. However, if we choose to look for Jesus in everything we do and remind our heart of His promises, there will be a light in our eyes and a lightness in our steps.

If everything that exited our mouth actually came to fruition, what would life look like? Would we propel ourselves in the direction of our dreams or steer ourselves down the path of insecurity and fear? We choose. Let's flip the script and believe that God is showing up for us; our heart can always remain hopeful.

Dear Jesus, thank You for helping us flip our perspective as we look for the ways You are moving on our behalf. We choose to speak words of life and truth today. In Jesus's name, amen.

Hope Redeems Wasted Time

These have come so that the proven genuineness
of your faith—of greater worth than gold,
which perishes even though refined by fire—
may result in praise, glory and honor
when Jesus Christ is revealed.

I PETER 1:7 NIV

Regret. The word alone is hard to read and say aloud. The truth is, we all have "wasted time" in life. This is not to say that God does not use even the consequences for our good; however, there are certainly moments, seasons, and even years of our life that we wish we could change. Our identity was compromised in one way or another. Whether it was a phase marked by rebellion, selfishness, pain, or insecurity, these windows of time plague our mind. We wonder to ourselves, "Have I wasted my life now?"

But God.

Only He is able to redeem our life and make every moment of those hard times be the exact recipe we need to be people of purpose. Our hope should never be in question because the Lord wastes nothing, even when we went in the opposite direction of what He commanded.

Whether we are in that hard place now, we just traveled through it, or it was years ago, we can let it be a catalyst to seeing God in a much more profound way. Because we have experienced the pit, we realize the depths of His grace. Our time with the Father is so much richer because we greater comprehend the fragility of our human existence. When our need is great, the One who meets our needs is at the forefront of our mind, increasing our trust in Him.

What we believe to have lost through our regrets, we can multiply in spiritual courage. Freedom is now our banner, and we have a redemption story to share. This urgency to be a disciple is a gift and a calling.

The Lord does not just redeem our wasted time by making us warriors in faith; He can multiply our efforts, extend any deadline, and make the sun stand still. When regrets do their best to convince us that shame is our song, we will sing back to them the melody of grace and march in victory with our Redeemer.

Dear Jesus, thank You for being our Rock and our Redeemer. You have restored our bones and covered us in grace. Give us the strength to stay on course and remind us that You make good of everything. In Jesus's name, amen.

Right Down the Rabbit Hole

You shall have no other gods before me.
You shall not make for yourself an image in the form
of anything in heaven above or on the earth beneath
or in the waters below.
EXODUS 20:3-4 NIV

Isn't it crazy how quickly our mind whirls? We were feeling good about our day and nothing felt wrong... and then we picked up our phone. Maybe it was the text that made us anxious or unsettled. Maybe it was the news article that discouraged our spirit. Maybe it was the Instagram picture that triggered that fear of being excluded. Maybe it was a call that completely threw us off and we can't seem to shake it.

Whatever it was, our peace feels out of reach now. So then what do we do? We keep searching, letting this little gadget in our hand completely control our mood, rob us of our time, and let our emotions govern our ability to rest. It is as if this tool has become a source of information overload, making our dispersed consciousness the perfect breeding ground for an anxious heart.

But what if, when we started to feel that defeated or discouraged feeling, we put down our phone and went to the throne? The moment we enter His presence, He will be waiting for us there. Familiar with the rat race and well-versed on the pressures of this world, He simply asks us to come.

To come and to be. To remind ourselves where our worth is from and who is in control of our life. He wants in on the big issues and the small details. He doesn't find our worries trivial, He just knows they're triggers—triggers to find our purpose in places and people other than Him—and therefore compromising our peace.

In our technology-driven world, we just have to remember why we are here and who is in charge. We aren't on the world's timeline. We do not hold the same priorities. We invest in a different kingdom, and sometimes we need the reminder that it's okay to feel that uneasiness. It's just not okay to stay there. Let's put down our phone and go to Him. Whatever it may be, when our mind begins to wander down the rabbit hole, let us recognize it, arrest our thoughts, and take them to the throne.

Dear Jesus, thank You for continually recalibrating our mind to align with Your Word. Will You keep us aware when we let the demands of our world get the best of our emotions? We are grateful for Your peace that satisfies our soul. In Jesus's name, amen.

Constant Course Correction

Repent, then, and turn to God,
so that your sins may be wiped out,
that times of refreshing may come from the Lord.
ACTS 3:19 NIV

"Rerouting...rerouting," we hear as we turn the wheel and head back toward our destination. Due to the distraction, we missed a turn and went too far. But because we knew our final destination and that it was plugged into the system, the GPS was able to reroute us despite our detours.

This experience is a familiar one for all of us. Just as our car needs this direction and rerouting, life is the same way. We are in want of constant course correction, and our faith helps us determine what road to take next—whether it be the popular way or not. As we pursue Jesus, we learn how to lean into Him and receive His instruction. When we struggle to obey or we get off course, we have the GPS of life—"God's Provision Service," as I like to call it—to help us return and realign ourselves in the direction intended for us.

Sometimes when we feel like hope is lost, it is because we have decided to continue in a direction that we know is not on our route. Our anxiety stems from the fact that our head is aware of the mistake and yet our heart continues down the path. We convince ourselves that we have traveled too far from our original destination and there is no point in turning around.

In these moments, we forget that the Lord's ability to course correct far exceeds our own. He is able to dispose of obstacles, make a way in the wilderness, and restore whatever we have lost. But we must first come to Him. Repentance literally means to turn around. This allows us to experience the redemption found in Him, which, in turn, produces the hope we crave.

Getting off course is inevitable, but the destiny of our life will be based on our swiftness to turn around and trust our GPS to lead the way. Jesus is a master at course correction, and when we let Him take the lead, our best is always yet to come.

Dear Jesus, thank You for never failing to help us get back on track, no matter how far we have strayed. You never left us. When we fear the consequences, remind our heart that repentance is the only way to hope. Our best is still ahead when we trust in You. In Jesus's name, amen.

Lasting Self-Care

For you formed my inward parts;
you knitted me together in my mother's womb.
I praise you, for I am fearfully and wonderfully made.
Wonderful are your works; my soul knows it very well.
PSALM 139:13-14 ESV

Wildly trendy and rampantly encouraged, "self-care" has become a phenomenon in our culture. Whether it be eating well, attending a yoga class, or getting more sleep at night, there are a million ways to practice it. The hope of self-care is that it will force us to be present in the moment, to soak in what's around us, and to implement practices that help us enjoy life. Our goal in disciplining ourselves in these habits is to work toward a life of peace.

But while most of these practices or habits are inherently good for us, we miss a key ingredient with any type of self-care when it ends in ourselves: self-care without soul-care only makes us comfortable in our hopelessness. In our rushed culture and hurried lifestyles, we have forgotten to stop and be grateful. We sacrifice and strive for the life we think we want, only to realize once we "arrive" that it still is not enough. While we may become physically fit and have perfect skin, peace cannot reside when experiencing pleasure is the goal of life. Self-care can only be a distraction from stress and a temporary fix when we are the center of the solution.

However, when we establish habits of treating our temple well and opening our eyes to the blessings around us so that we can glorify God? That is a self-care plan that lasts. Whether we realize it or not, the fit body was a plus, but it was never the true goal. We crave fulfillment. We deeply desire peace. We were wired with eternity in mind, so pleasing ourself will never rid us of the yearning we have to find the real meaning of life: following Jesus.

So, yes, we should wake up earlier and eat better. We should be more intentional in our quiet time. But in all that we do and in all the changes we implement, may it be for Him. When we drink from the well of Living Water, we will experience the greatest pleasure we could ever know: peace in Jesus.

Dear Jesus, thank You for giving us the body, mind, soul, spirit, and heart that You did. Show us how to pursue You in the ways we tend to ourselves and the world around us. Remove our selfishness and set our eyes on You. In Jesus's name, amen.

Hope of Imperfect Progress

Not that I have already obtained all this,
or have already arrived at my goal,
but I press on to take hold of that
for which Christ Jesus took hold of me.

PHILIPPIANS 3:12 NIV

We can all think of something we are relatively good at. For some of us it's cooking, and for others it might be baseball. For some it's playing a musical instrument, and for others it's designing a home. We all have our hobbies and interests that we enjoy, but we were not always good at them.

Even when we had a knack for whatever it is we like to do, the journey to doing it well required diligence and practice. We had to show up and continue to show up even when it required us to learn things we didn't want to learn. The progress was imperfect because that's exactly what progress is—the continuance of something that has not yet been perfected or made complete.

How many hobbies would we have if we refused to try again after seeing our imperfections? Probably none. And how many promotions would we receive in our workplace if we became frustrated with the gap between where we are and where we should be? Most likely zero. We show up each day with the hope of being just a teeny tiny bit better. Even if we take one step back in one direction, we will learn what not to do—and therefore still move forward.

There is great hope in taking one step each day, proving to ourselves that we are consistent, reliable, and capable of everyday progress. As long as we can commit to the process that is required for anything good to grow, we can climb any mountain put in front of us. Success does not stem from what we do *occasionally*; it comes from what we do *consistently*. How are we showing up? Do we look like people who have hope in God and His plans? Are we willing to risk our pride for the growth found in imperfect progress?

Allowing ourselves to be refined and carrying forward imperfectly gives us the permission to grow.

Dear Jesus, thank You for being a God who never expects perfection but simply asks us to surrender our all. Help us to be okay with growing slowly or different than expected because we know that our hope is in You. You make beautiful things out of the dust. In Jesus's name, amen.

Redeeming Our Roots

Rooted and built up in him and established in the faith,
just as you were taught, abounding in thanksgiving.
COLOSSIANS 2:7 ESV

Have you ever seen how bamboo grows? It is rapid. Continuous. All bamboo cells need to grow is to fill up with water, which happens quickly. It is also a colony plant, meaning that more plants are created by using the energy from existing plants and expanding the root structure. Bamboo grows over gates and fences and can be found in the crevices and breaks of sidewalks. If growing near the foundation of a building, it can aggravate any breaks or cracks that are around.

Much like bamboo, there are some struggles that can seep into our life and wreak havoc on everything they touch. One struggle that grows quickly and without mercy is self-rejection. We all struggle with this in some facet, whether it be our insecurities in the workplace, our self-conscious approach to establishing relationships, our struggles with family, or hatred of our own personal appearance.

What began as our desire to lose weight turns into an obsession, which manifests into an eating disorder and begins to consume our entire life. What started as our weariness to make new friends turned into isolating ourselves, which has grown into complete anxiety in social situations. Self-rejection feeds off our previous insecurity and uses our vulnerability as a catalyst to grow its roots. Its main goal is to overtake our foundation.

In order for bamboo to be removed from an area, its roots must be destroyed. Self-rejection is the same way—if we think we can control the habit or experience healing without tending to the deep roots, we are deceiving ourselves. But when we let the Lord rip out those roots and replace them with His truth? We give room for the good stuff to grow.

And the beauty of God? No root is too deep for Him. He created us and He called it "very good." As we watch the sunset, let us remember that the same God who created the beauty around us also created us. When we see His hand in all that surrounds us, we must remember that we are His prized masterpiece.

Dear Jesus, thank You for establishing our worth long before we came to be. Will You help us find the roots that must be removed and give us the courage to do so? Make us uncomfortable so that we can look more like You. In Jesus's name, amen.

"Who Do You Say That I Am?"

In the same way, let your light shine before others,
that they may see your good deeds
and glorify your Father in heaven.
MATTHEW 5:16 NIV

How would we have responded if Jesus had asked us this question like He did the disciples: "Who do you say that I am?"

"You are the Lord!" we would stammer, struggling to get the words out that we have told ourselves we believe. "You are the Great I Am!" we say. Because He is this, we know.

But when looking at our life and assessing the way we carry out our beliefs, what would be the honest response to that question? If life was a movie without sound and the movie answered this question about who we believe God to be, what would it say?

This is why it is so important to take the time to be still and to get alone with Him—what does our life say about the Jesus we claim to serve? Honest reflection requires vulnerability, and this vulnerability demands the need to be still. Oftentimes the movement going on around us and the commotion going on within us keep us from being honest about how we answer this question.

The truth is, how we answer this question brings light to every other situation, perspective, and belief in our life. If we say He is trustworthy but fear dictates how we make decisions, do we really believe Him to be trustworthy? If we say He is good but our doubt prevents us from stepping forward into our calling, do we really believe Him to be trustworthy? If we say He is our God but we spend more time with every other thing in life, do we really believe Him to be God?

He does not demand perfection. He does not expect that our actions will always reflect His kindness, and in every moment it doesn't, His grace is sufficient. But He wants us to be honest in this answer, with ourselves and with Him, because He knows that it is in our belief of Him that we develop our belief in everything else.

May we live keeping this question in mind. Who do we say that He is? The Almighty and The Great I Am.

Dear Jesus, thank You that You are exactly who You say You are at all times. We want our life to reflect Your heart and be people of truth. Give us boldness. Help us to be firm in our following so that others know we trust only in You. In Jesus's name, amen.

A World of Image Bearers

*And to put on the new self, created after the likeness of
God in true righteousness and holiness.*
EPHESIANS 4:24 ESV

What would it be like if we spent less time working to perfect our own image and spent more time speaking out His perfection in others? How would the world look differently if we were less image-conscious but were more conscious of the image of God in others?

We would find refuge together, pointing out the ways God is being made strong in our weaknesses. We would have our eternal home in mind, imagining gatherings in heaven, and our attention would be on spreading God's love. We would avoid comparison, allowing our focus to be the ways in which we individually reflect His grandeur. Differences would be delightful and appreciation for one another's heart would take priority over the coveting of their appearance.

But how do we do this when we have been trained to do otherwise? We learn a new way and decide to consistently practice it in life, that's how. When we look in the mirror to get ready for the day, we speak words of life over the person we are and the life we have been given. When we approach our schedule, we operate with discernment in how we spend our time and whom we place ourselves near. When we see something beautiful or special in someone around us, we open our mouth and we tell them. The more our radar is "on" for recognizing Him in ourselves and those around us, the more frequently our eyes will notice that He is there.

And most importantly? We spend time with the One who made us. When we have questions or concerns with how we are made or why we look or feel the way we do, we bring them to Him. We ask Him to explain all the things that make us, us. Much like our own personal experience with art or design, the more time we spend with the Creator, the more we appreciate the masterpiece. Soaking up time with Jesus and receiving His love is the best way we can learn to love ourselves and others. As we hear His voice and witness His provision and power for ourselves, the more we will recognize His image in every moment we experience.

Dear Jesus, thank You for creating us in the image of You. When You look at us, You see Jesus, perfect and whole. Help us to be diligent in looking for your beauty within ourselves and those around us. We are Your masterpiece, fearfully and wonderfully made. In Jesus's name, amen.

"*Joy is not the absence of darkness. Joy is confidence that the darkness will lift.*"

REBEKAH LYONS

A God of Systems

This is what the Sovereign LORD says:
Look! I am going to put breath into you
and make you live again!
EZEKIEL 37:5 NLT

The circulatory system. The endocrine system. The digestive system. The ecosystem. The solar system. The transportation system. The water system. Systems are everywhere and have been since the creation of the earth. God loves systems. He is a God of order and function. He creates rhythms that allow the world to flow in the most effective manner and adapt to all it may endure. He created the human body with twelve different systems that work in tandem and allow us to move, live, and have our being.

Would it not also make sense that God would want us to pay attention to these systems? The routines we hold, the way we organize our days, and the way our mind and body respond to these systems—all of these matter greatly. They affect our ability to receive His Word and respond in a way that honors Him.

We all know that when we want ourselves or

others to calm down, we encourage deep breaths. We emphasize the importance of slowing down. We speak to the necessity of putting all else aside and focusing on the here and now—being present to the need rather than being anxious about the before and after possibilities of the moment. This is us recognizing the systems that the Lord put into place. Our physical body needs the break of pace. When life is whirling around us or overwhelmed feelings take over, stress becomes our fuel and our system gets completely out of whack. Exhausted. Burnt out. We see what needs to be done, but there is no steam left in the engine.

Systems were created for efficiency, adaptability, and longevity. God does not slow us down to prevent us from getting where we want to go; He slows us down so that we can remember where we should be going. While *we* believe we will break if we stop, He knows we will break if we don't.

Let us be aware of the way we were created, remembering that every part of the rhythm is necessary to be at its best.

Dear Jesus, thank You for being a God of order and of freedom and of grace. Remind us that efficiency is not separate from rest or joy. We delight in walking in Your rhythm as You lead our way. In Jesus's name, amen.

The Walk to the Cross

Then He said to them all:
"Whoever wants to be My disciple
must deny themselves and
take up their cross daily and follow Me."
LUKE 9:23 NIV

We ask, "Lord, where are You?" "Lord, what am I supposed to do with this?" Frustrated and doubtful, we move our feet forward and see the cross in the distance. As we notice the well-traveled dirt beneath our feet and feel the weight of our world lessen in strength, we remember His sacrifice. As we set down our bags and lift up our head, we see Him there. "Oh," we remember, "You have done it all for me."

Hope is what allows us to believe again and again. It is the force that helps us show up when we don't want to and is the stamina behind our persistence. Hope propels our feet forward when we do not want to step. We curse our struggle until we realize that our white flag was the marker of our victory, not our defeat.

The only way that we can see our struggles as

setups for His faithfulness is if we believe that the purpose of our life is to intimately understand and share the hope we claim to have. If we recognize our value as anything but, we will continue to strive, attain, and wear ourselves out. What we thought would restore us makes our bones dry and our spirit weary. And so we return to the cross, the only place that has accepted our brokenness exactly as it comes, with our heart beginning to remember the One who gave everything so that our life could be something.

And it is then that we stop wondering why we have to walk all that way. We begin to question Him less when He directs us down a rocky road. The walk to the cross—we must always make it. Every day. And when our legs feel unsure and tired, we must ask Him to carry us there. The remembrance of His sacrifice is always our way to hope.

Dear Jesus, thank You for reminding our soul that we must take up our cross daily. Your sacrifice preserved our life—may we keep that at the forefront of our mind. You are our hope. In Jesus's name, amen.

Sustaining Abundance

And God is able to bless you abundantly,
so that in all things at all times, having all that you need,
you will abound in every good work.
II CORINTHIANS 9:8 NIV

What do we imagine when we think of abundance? Probably an overwhelming amount of something, a heap of resources or a jar overflowing with way more than it needs.

While this picture does describe abundance in a tangible sense, it forgets the most important attribute of true abundance. When Scripture talks about the Lord blessing us, it is referenced in the same context as the urgency to give. The only way for us to "abound in every good work" is for us to wholeheartedly serve Jesus in the way that we give to those around us. Jesus fulfills every single one of our needs in the highest and most efficient capacity, and then we are given more.

Think about those times when the soul really feels alive—whether it be serving at a homeless shelter, showing up at a friend's house with cookies, or giving to a cause that is near to our heart. It is these times when the magic of purpose is sparked and we witness the brilliance of the human spirit. This is what God has always hoped for His children, that we would taste and see the goodness of the Lord and that we would spread it like wildfire. While the state of abundance is the surplus of something, the attainment of abundance occurs through giving that surplus.

When the harvest is plenty, it feels easy to give. The resources are there. We know our needs will be met. But when the call to give feels sacrificial, almost as if He's asking us to give over and beyond our capabilities? That is when we must go back to this same Scripture of abundance, knowing that the Lord will provide for our needs, satisfy our soul, and help us move forward in all we were created to do.

How do we sustain abundance? We learn that the fountain from which we drink is dependable. And we remind our soul that the magic we keep looking for has never been found in anything we own but rather in whom we follow.

Dear Jesus, thank You for being a God of abundance and for giving us a full life. Will You help us to have open hands and a generous heart, remembering that the greatest riches are those we give away? Thank You for always taking care of us. In Jesus's name, amen.

Identity-Driven Purpose

For we are God's handiwork, created in Christ Jesus to do
good works, which God prepared in advance for us to do.
EPHESIANS 2:10 NIV

What is the one question we all ask and wonder whether it is true for our life: "Am I living a life of purpose?" We all crave knowing that when we wake up in the morning and put our feet on the ground, the next twelve hours are not a waste of time. We want to be people of wisdom who operate in obedience and make a difference in this world.

While the Lord loves that we desire to do good work and move His kingdom forward, we often get caught up in this vortex. We spend so much time questioning whether our life is significant that we forget where our significance comes from. Subconsciously, we have taken the desire to live a purpose-driven life and made it our idol, obsessing over what we do and where we go. Our purpose begins to drive our identity, and we begin to desire the affirmation more than we desire to simply serve Jesus.

But when our identity drives our purpose? Life stops feeling like this elusive puzzle we must figure out in order not to miss it. We spend time with our Maker and we are reminded that we are chosen, called, and worthy. We understand that as people who know the truth, it is our responsibility to share God's love with others. We receive the gift of His lavished love, and our life naturally flows in response. Because we know who we are, we know what we should do. We do not consume ourselves with being well-known in our service; rather, we obey and simply do as He asks.

We walk across the street and serve our neighbor. We refuse to gossip about those who annoy us. We create intentional moments of gathering to talk about His faithfulness. We give our resources and our energy to those in need. We fulfill our purpose in the moment and trust that our God will move the puzzle pieces as He sees fit.

When we walk in our God-given identity as children of the King, wasting our life is not a possibility. He has mighty plans for His mountain movers; they only must take one step at a time.

Dear Jesus, thank You for establishing our identity firmly in You. As we approach our day and our schedule, let us follow as You lead. We choose to find our significance in You, serving others as You did, out of love and obedience, not recognition. In Jesus's name, amen.

Who Has the Microphone?

Let the word of Christ dwell in you richly in all wisdom,
teaching and admonishing one another in psalms
and hymns and spiritual songs,
singing with grace in your hearts to the Lord.
COLOSSIANS 3:16 NKJV

Since we were in the womb, we have had people speaking into and over our life. As small children, we heard the words of our family and friends and whatever culture surrounded us. Then we became adults. A new opportunity presented itself when we became responsible for the places and people we surround ourselves with. The question became: who is holding our microphone?

Many times we assume that the microphone is innately passed to whoever wants to tell us their opinion about our potential. We hear their words and weave their opinions into the fabric of our identity. We believe that our family and friends love us, so they should have rights to the microphone.

The truth is, we pass our microphone incessantly, vying for the affirmation of others. While some truth is expressed, we allow the opinions of others and their interpretation of who we are to cloud the view we have of ourselves. We place their opinions on the same level as the Word of God and we accept their words of truth. But the only person capable of interpreting the depths of our soul, knowing our potential, and speaking life into dry bones is Jesus. He instructs us to seek wise counsel, but when the voices of others do not align with His Word, He tells us to give Him back the microphone. What does He say about us? What is the truth on this subject?

Who are we trusting to provide feedback on the things that are important to us? Are we giving a voice to the critics in our life who sit in the cheap seats with a bird's-eye view of what is really going on in our heart? When we give Jesus the microphone, we place ourselves in a position to hear the direct truth about who we are in Him. When we let Him be the audible voice in our mind, we exhibit self-control and peace. When we seek wise counsel that follows after Him, we allow ourselves to receive wisdom and teaching that aligns with His truth. Who is holding our microphone? And how are we handling the responsibility of speaking into others?

Dear Jesus, thank You for the gift of Your affirmation and truth that You pour into us. Help us chase Your will, not the agreement of those around us. We ask that You give and take away the microphone from whomever You see fit in our life. In Jesus's name, amen.

A Teachable Spirit

Hold on to instruction, do not let it go;
guard it well, for it is your life.
PROVERBS 4:13 NIV

We are forever students in this thing called life. We are learning how to navigate new seasons, walk through patches of disappointment, steward the relationships that have been placed in our life, and be people who look like Jesus. And when it comes to the school of life, honor roll is determined a little differently.

Instead of it being about our performance and our abilities, the Lord looks at the humility our heart holds. He does not ask that we be perfect; He asks that we be pupils of His perfect Word. Mistakes are automatic because our humanity is irrevocable on this side of heaven; however, it is in our desire to be teachable that the Lord delights in His children.

When we have a teachable spirit, we allow hope to be cultivated. When we take the time to read His Word and sit under His teaching, we position ourselves in a place to understand what hope really means. This does not mean that when we walk outside His classroom, the chaos surrounding us will drastically change. In fact, becoming more like Jesus and doing what He asks will increase our empathy and make us more aware of the chaos outside us. But the inside? The humility of our heart will have laid the foundation for peace to be our posture no matter what we are enduring. Being teachable receives instruction as breeding ground for improvement rather than personal offense.

A teachable spirit understands its position. We assume our role as daughters and sons of the Most High King. This means that we know the way in which we should go, and we exert our authority in walking with Him. We heed His instruction and listen to His voice, especially when it contradicts our own. Placing ourselves and our focus on His promises is the wisest thing we can do. It is our pathway to success and our foundation for peace.

May we humble ourselves and honor Him in all we do, realizing our place as students and being diligent with our time, resources, and gifts. The world needs us to be teachable so that we can be the leaders He has called us to be.

Dear Jesus, thank You for giving us a teachable spirit. We choose to be still and sit under Your instruction as we let wisdom guide our life. Humble us when we want to become the teacher, and make Your authority known to us in every moment. In Jesus's name, amen.

Margin Multiplies

He has shown you, O man, what is good;
and what does the LORD require of you but to do justly,
to love mercy, and to walk humbly with your God?
MICAH 6:8 NKJV

Isn't it crazy how almost any job or activity can take up the entire amount of time we give it? In other words, margin is not created by accident. When it comes to our jobs, the more space and time we allow it to dictate, the more we will prioritize it. We hope and often assume that by giving more of ourselves, we will receive a promotion or increase our territory. The dedication will be worth it. Parenting—and relationships of any kind—certainly follow this same mind-set. When it comes to relationships, they can occupy our entire headspace if we give them permission.

Wherever our focus, there will always be new land to discover, problems to solve, goals to attain, or standards we have not reached. While this means limitless possibilities, it also means that life will not be the one knocking on our door and asking us if we have the built-in margin necessary. Margin is something we must schedule, prioritize, and treat just as seriously. Sometimes we worry that if we do schedule this intentional time of solitude, stillness, or air in our schedules to "just be," we will compromise our other areas of attention. However, what we do not realize, until it is too late, is that if we do not demand margin from ourselves, the other areas of our life naturally suffer.

By allowing ourselves to have true free time, our heart remembers what we naturally enjoy. We are far more inclined to take a walk around the neighborhood, read a book at our favorite coffee shop, or get back our green thumb. Our passion is reignited and we give ourselves space to think, to receive instruction from God, to learn more about our gifts, and to remember the purpose behind this whole thing called life.

Margin multiplies itself—always. Any time we spend with God doing whatever it is that we love to do is never wasted. We become more efficient employees, more compassionate friends, more patient parents, more respectful romantic partners, and more intentional, aware people.

Dear Jesus, thank You for creating the gift of time and for guiding us in how to spend that time. Show us how to create margin in life and teach us how to be still with You. Thank You for multiplying the time we give You and guiding us down paths of diligence. In Jesus's name, amen.

Action Over Intention

For the word of God is living and active and sharper than
any two-edged sword, and piercing as far as the division
of soul and spirit, of both joints and marrow, and able to
judge the thoughts and intentions of the heart.

HEBREWS 4:12 NASB

For the most part, we all have good intentions. We want to be healthy, intentionally serve others, and remember our friends' birthdays. We want to show up for our kids, be good friends, and pursue our dreams.

Who wouldn't want all these things? But we can look back on our life and see how far intentions have gotten us. Some things have panned out as hoped, and others not so much. We have a large file full of "dreams" that have remained so because we have put little to no action or thought behind pursuing them. We are good at deceiving ourselves; we want to make something happen, but our priorities and schedule do not line up with our words. When we begin to align our actions with our intentions, we get results.

Many of us fall prey to claiming that we want a slower life, but we do not take the steps necessary to actually slowing down. Whether that be decreasing our number of commitments, changing our sleep schedule, or putting our phone away, we must be people of follow-through. The reason so many of us become insecure or worried about this is because we no longer trust ourselves with the claims we make. We have expressed desires for so long, but we have not shown up and worked to make them a reality.

Stillness with God? It only happens with action, not intention. Our desire to give Him priority and space to speak to us is not enough; we must be disciplined in our coming to His throne. We all know that impact is not possible with intention alone. But when we attach our time and our resources and set excuses aside, we initiate helpful habits that keep our heart accountable. When intention aligns with action, our confidence grows and we are reminded that what we value and what we invest in will increase, gain momentum, and cause true impact.

Dear Jesus, thank You for giving us a proactive spirit and an attitude of excellence. We want to be people of action not merely intention. Help us line up what we do with what we say and who You are. Thank You for always keeping Your promises to us—we want to be dependable like You. In Jesus's name, amen.

The Hope of Joseph

As for you, you meant evil against me,
but God meant it for good in order to bring about
this present result, to preserve many people alive.

GENESIS 50:20 NASB

When reading the story of Joseph in the Bible, it's important to not strip humanity from the story. Joseph was human just like us; the trauma and hardship he experienced are hard to comprehend. He was hated by his brothers because he was favored by his father. He became a slave and was then thrown into prison. However, amid so much intense struggle, the Bible says over and over again that the favor of God was with Joseph. When Joseph was a young boy, he had dreams about becoming a leader. From the outside looking in, his story seemed hopeless at times. A leader? He was a slave and then a prisoner. It turns out that every part of Joseph's story was preparing him to become the second-most powerful man in the world, below Pharaoh.

Joseph did not turn his back or forget his dreams. He resisted temptation and clung to the Lord's promises. His faith was continually tested and God continually delivered, preparing his heart for each step. It is because of this that Joseph was able to offer grace instead of anger, give obedience instead of bitterness, and walk in hope instead of defeat. It is easy to talk about our hope when favor seems to be upon us, but how do we respond when we feel forgotten?

We serve a really, really big God. Just as He delivered Joseph, He uses the tests in life to display His glory to the watching world. When circumstances are far less than ideal, we can confidently say, "This is preparation for something better." The story of Joseph reveals two very important things: God's plans will always supersede our own, and His plans are rooted in a much greater purpose. His glory is being revealed in our hardship. He is making all things new. He is present in our darkness—and where His presence is, hope is alive.

Dear Jesus, thank You for Your ability to use any and every situation for our good and Your glory. We place our hope and our joy in Your presence. Thank You for being near. Open our eyes like You did for Joseph, so that we may see the workings of Your hands even in the hardest places. In Jesus's name, amen.

Get Silent; Listen Up

My sheep hear my voice, and I know them, and they follow me. I give them eternal life, and they will never perish, and no one will snatch them out of my hand.
JOHN 10:27–28 ESV

Have you ever noticed how the words *silent* and *listen* contain the exact same letters? If you rearrange *silent*, the word *listen* is formed, and vice versa. Thinking about this, it does not seem to be a coincidence. How do we listen? When in conversation with others, and in everyday life situations, it is no secret that the act of listening has become more difficult. We believe we are all capable of multitasking even in the most urgent of situations. We have music in the background, a meal cooking in the oven, and a to-do list going in our head, all while trying to have a serious conversation with someone. This productivity complex of always needing to feel effective has compromised our ability to put away everything and simply listen.

But if we are being honest with ourselves, when is clarity possible? Do we tend to listen better when there are no distractions around us? Of course. In order to hear the direction of our heavenly Father and to better understand His heart, silence is required. And silence requires stillness. Sometimes the loudest words are not those being said to us but those we are telling ourselves. We rush from one thing to another, clawing for some form of guidance, but what the Lord is really asking of us is to get still and lean into Him.

The more time we spend listening to His voice, the more we recognize it. We are His sheep, His prized possessions, the focus of all of His attention...and He desires to lead us into pleasant spaces. Our rightful place is in His grasp, and no one and nothing can snatch us away from that safe place—how comforting that is! In this safe haven, we come to know the hope of His heart, and it gives us that same hope for our life. Silence and stillness give way for us to listen, and when we do, our momentary troubles lighten and His strength is infused into our being. May we remember that it is often when we allow ourselves to get quiet that God does His loudest work in us.

Dear Jesus, thank You for reminding us of the importance of getting still and silent so that we may listen well. Help us to have the confidence of hearing Your voice, and give us the courage to follow through with Your instructions. Calm our heart as we lean into You. In Jesus's name, amen.

"God has infinite attention to spare for each one of us. You are as much alone with Him as if you were the only being He had ever created."

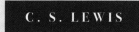

C. S. LEWIS

LIVE YOUR FAITH

Dear Friend,

This book was prayerfully crafted with you, the reader, in mind—every word, every sentence, every page— was thoughtfully written, designed, and packaged to encourage you...right where you are this very moment. At DaySpring, our vision is to see every person experience the life-changing message of God's love. So, as we worked through rough drafts, design changes, edits, and details, we prayed for you to deeply experience His unfailing love, indescribable peace, and pure joy. It is our sincere hope that through these Truth-filled pages your heart will be blessed, knowing that God cares about you—your desires and disappointments, your challenges and dreams.

He knows. He cares. He loves you unconditionally.

BLESSINGS!
THE DAYSPRING BOOK TEAM

Additional copies of this book and
other DaySpring titles can be purchased
at fine bookstores everywhere.
Order online at dayspring.com
or
by phone at 1-877-751-4347

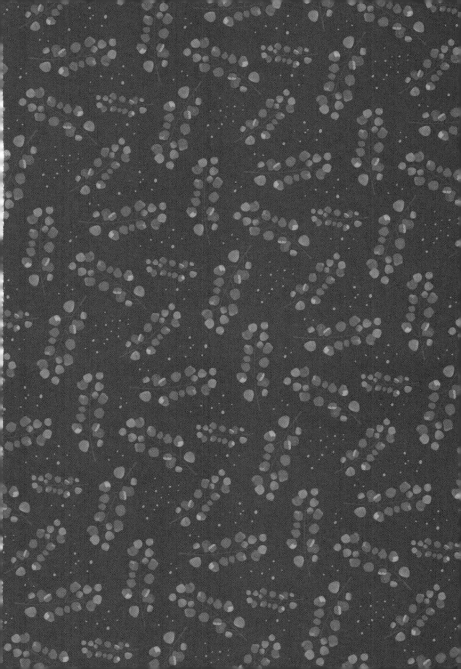

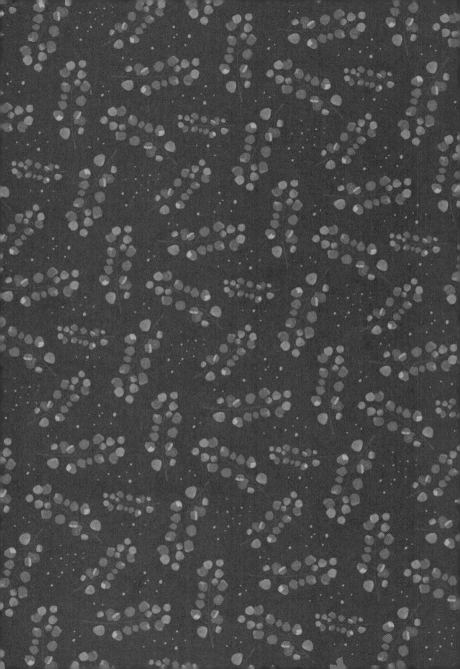